The Fatal Fortress

'Singapore, the Gibraltar of the East'

Daily Express

To Nicholas, Jessica, Andrew and Sue

The Fatal Fortress

The Guns and Fortifications of Singapore 1819–1956

Bill Clements

Pen & Sword
MILITARY

First published in Great Britain in 2016 by
Pen & Sword Military
an imprint of
Pen & Sword Books Ltd
47 Church Street
Barnsley
South Yorkshire
S70 2AS

ISBN 978 1 47382 956 5

A CIP catalogue record for this book is available from the British
Library

Typeset in Ehrhardt by
Mac Style Ltd, Bridlington, East Yorkshire
Printed and bound in the UK by CPI Group (UK) Ltd,
Croydon, CR0 4YY

Pen & Sword Books Ltd incorporates the imprints of Pen & Sword
Archaeology, Atlas, Aviation, Battleground, Discovery, Family
History, History, Maritime, Military, Naval, Politics, Railways, Select,
Transport, True Crime, and Fiction, Frontline Books, Leo Cooper,
Praetorian Press, Seaforth Publishing and Wharncliffe.

For a complete list of Pen & Sword titles please contact
PEN & SWORD BOOKS LIMITED
47 Church Street, Barnsley, South Yorkshire, S70 2AS, England
E-mail: enquiries@pen-and-sword.co.uk
Website: www.pen-and-sword.co.uk

Contents

Preface

Having lived in the Far East and travelled extensively there for many years, I have long been fascinated by the fortifications of the British Empire, Singapore being one of the largest and, indeed, the most infamous. The subject of the Singapore fortifications, which date from the mid-nineteenth century, appears to me to be very under-researched. Much has been written about the Malayan Campaign in the Second World War, and the actual battle for Singapore has been well covered by various historians, but books on the physical defences of Singapore are few in number and rarely consider the fortifications in detail.

However, two recent publications, *Between Two Oceans: a military history of Singapore from the first settlement to final British withdrawal* by Murfett, Miksic, Farrell and Chiang, and *Did Singapore Have to Fall? Churchill and the impregnable fortress* by Hack and Blackburn, have considered the subject. The former authors have looked at the political aspects of the fortification of Singapore in great detail, while the latter concentrate on the fortifications constructed to defend the island immediately prior to the Second World War. I must acknowledge a debt to these authors as their research has assisted me greatly.

As always when writing a book, I have been assisted by a number of people. Peter Stubbs has been unstinting in his help by answering a number of queries, and in providing photographs. His website *Fort Siloso (www.fortsiloso.com)* contains a comprehensive description of the majority of Singapore's forts and batteries from the 1880s onwards. I am also grateful to Martin Brown, who drew the maps for the book, and to John Roberts for permitting me to use his drawing of the 15in gun. Michael Saunders in Penang provided me with a most comprehensive guide to the remaining fortifications and British military relics in Singapore, and Charles Blackwood has been most helpful in preparing many of the photographs for publication. Lynne Copping very kindly provided the 1950s photograph of the Silingsing Battery.

Mrs Margaret Pinsent very kindly proofread the manuscript for me, and her eagle eye ensured that a host of grammatical errors and the frequently unnecessary repetition of words was avoided. As a result, I believe this is a very much more readable book than it might otherwise have been.

Most of my research has been carried out at the National Archives at Kew and at the British Library at St Pancras. As always, the staff of these two great institutions have been unfailingly helpful. My thanks go also to the staff of the National Army Museum in London and Stevenage; to the staff of the Royal Engineers Library at Chatham; to Paul Evans of the James Clavell Library at the Royal Artillery Museum 'Firepower' and to George Chamier, my editor.

I have made every effort to find the copyright holder of each of the pictures and plans used to illustrate this book, and to obtain the appropriate permission to publish. However, if I have unwittingly infringed an owner's copyright I can only apologise and say that I have tried to find the owner but failed.

I hope this book, despite its perhaps somewhat specialized subject matter, will be of interest to a wide variety of readers, and that it will give the reader an insight into the complicated, and frequently convoluted, history of colonial defence planning.

Bill Clements
Stamford, 2016

Chapter 1

The Founding of Singapore

Singapore, a lozenge-shaped island, lies some 85 miles (130km) north of the Equator at the tip of the Malay Peninsula. Today the island, together with some sixty or more smaller islands and islets, forms the modern city state of the Republic of Singapore. The island is 272 square miles (716 square km) in area, and its highest natural point is Bukit Timah which stands at 545ft (166m). The main island is some 25 miles (40km) in length and 14 miles (22km) at its greatest breadth. To the north it is separated from Malaysia by the Strait of Johore and to the south from the closest Indonesian territory, the Riau Islands, by the Singapore Strait. There is a natural harbour on the south side of the island and deep water in the Strait of Johore. In addition, a line of low hills overlook what was the early nineteenth century settlement of Singapura, and these were subsequently named by the British 'Government Hill', 'Mount Palmer' and 'Mount Faber', this last having been named in 1846 after a Captain Charles Edward Faber of the Madras Engineers, who built a road to a signal station at the top of the hill.

Off the southern extremity of Singapore lies the island of Blakang Mati, now known as Sentosa Island, a triangular-shaped island 2½ miles (4 km) in length and 800yds (740m) in average breadth. The highest point on the island is Mount Serapong near its eastern end at about 300ft (92m). Between Blakang Mati and Singapore Island runs a channel with a minimum depth of six fathoms, forming a fine natural harbour previously known as the New Harbour. Near the eastern entrance to the New Harbour there is a smaller, irregularly shaped island, Pulau Brani, the highest point of which is approximately 170ft (52m).

In 1819, when Sir Stamford Raffles set foot on the island of Singapore, it was of little importance either commercially or strategically, and sparsely populated. Only a small population of fishermen, who were nominally under the jurisdiction of the Sultan of Riau and the local *Temenggong* (nobleman), inhabited the island. However, it had not always been such a quiet backwater. Known as Tumasik as early as AD 1025, it was already an independent city and port in the thirteenth century and, according to Chinese documents, repulsed a Siamese naval expedition in the early fourteenth. The island was also frequently referred to as 'Singapura', a Sanskrit name meaning 'Lion City'. The fact that Tumasik had, in its day, been an important city and trading port could be seen from the remains of defences that were described by John Crawfurd, later to become Resident of Singapore.

Sir Thomas Stamford Bingley Raffles by James Thomson, 1824 engraving. (*National Portrait Gallery, London*)

Crawfurd visited Singapore in February 1822 as a member of an embassy to the Courts of Siam and Indo-China. He recorded in his journal:

> I walked this morning round the walls and limits of the ancient town of Singapore, for such in reality had been the site of our modern settlement. It was bounded to the east by the sea, to the north by a wall, and to the west by a salt creek or inlet of the sea. The inclosed [sic] space is a plain, ending in a hill of considerable extent, and a hundred and fifty feet in height. The whole is a kind of triangle, of which the base is the sea-side, about a mile in length. The wall, which is about sixteen feet in breadth at its base, and at present about eight or nine feet in height, runs very near a mile from the sea-coast to the base of the hill until it meets a salt marsh. As long as it continues in the plain, it is skirted by a little rivulet running at the foot of it, and forming a kind of moat; and where it attains the elevated side of the hill, there are apparent the remains of a dry ditch. On the western side, which extends from the

termination of the wall to the sea, the distance, like that of the northern side, is very near a mile. This last has the natural and strong defence of a salt marsh, overflown at high-water, and of a deep and broad creek and marsh. In the wall there were no traces of embrasures or loop-holes; and neither on the sea-side, nor on that side skirted by the creek and marsh, is there any appearance whatever of artificial defences. We may conclude from these circumstances, that the works of Singapore were not intended against fire-arms, or any attack by sea; or that if the latter, the inhabitants considered themselves strong in their naval force, and, therefore, thought any other defences in that quarter superfluous.[1]

By 1819, however, despite its strategic location, Tumasik (Singapura) was no longer even a shadow of its former self; only a length of ruined wall and a number of carved blocks of stone, including one on which were the remains of an inscription, remained to give any indication of its former glory.

British interest in Singapore resulted directly from trade between the Honourable East India Company (HEIC) and China. Since the sixteenth century there had been rivalry between the English and Dutch over possession of the Spice Islands of modern-day Indonesia. The Dutch had been the winners in the competition for possession of these islands and, apart from temporary occupation of Batavia from 1811 to 1816, the only foothold the British retained there was the small fever-ridden outpost of Bencoolen on the south-eastern coast of the island of Sumatra.

However, the rivalry between the two nations continued, and in 1786 the British established themselves on the island of Penang, half way up the western coast of the Malay Peninsula, which they renamed Prince of Wales Island, its main port being the newly established post of Georgetown. The reason for the acquisition of Penang was to provide a staging post for HEIC ships on their way to and from China. The China tea trade was the most important business carried out by the HEIC, and the Company's ships had, of necessity, to pass through either the Malacca Strait or the Strait of Sunda on their way to and from China. In the days of sail, voyages to China were dependent on the two annual monsoon winds, the north-east and the south-west. Captains of East Indiamen planned their outward voyage to coincide with the south-west monsoon as they rounded the tip of the Malay Peninsula which would carry them through the Strait of Malacca, then sailed back from Canton with the north-east monsoon.

As trade with China increased towards the end of the eighteenth and into the early nineteenth century, the HEIC realized that a base was needed close to the Strait of Malacca to enable their ships to replenish their stores and to counter Dutch control of the strait. The existing stations, Georgetown on Prince of Wales Island and Fort Marlborough (Bencoolen) on Sumatra, were poorly situated, and Malacca, which had been seized in 1798, although better placed geographically, was returned to the Dutch in 1816. Indeed, it was the possession by the Dutch of Malacca on the Malay Peninsula and Batavia on the island of Java that placed them in the powerful position of being able to control the strategically important Strait of Malacca and, potentially, to close the strait to HEIC vessels should they so wish.

With this as the background, Sir Stamford Raffles, the acknowledged founder of modern Singapore, appears on the scene. Raffles had started his career as a junior clerk in the HEIC in 1795 and, in 1805, through influence, was posted to Prince of Wales Island as the Assistant Secretary. He quickly proved to be an able administrator and soon became known to the Governor General in Calcutta, Lord Minto. Raffles had come to the Governor-General's attention through his close friend John Leyden, who had arrived in Penang in 1805 and been befriended by Raffles and his wife Olivia. Leyden subsequently left Penang for Calcutta where, because of his fluency in languages, he became intimate with Lord Minto and acted as interpreter for the Governor General.

By 1811 the French had been strengthening their position in Java, which they had obtained as a result of the accession of Louis I, Napoleon's brother, to the throne of the Netherlands in 1806. From that date the Royal Navy had been maintaining a blockade of the major ports of Java, paralyzing the French and Dutch trade between the islands and, incidentally, seriously affecting Penang's trade. At this time Raffles, acting Secretary for Prince of Wales Island, hearing of plans for the capture of Mauritius in the Indian ocean from the French, put forward his own ideas for the capture of Java, together with a memorandum that contained all the intelligence he had obtained regarding the island and its garrison. Lord Minto approved the proposal and in 1810 passed the planning of the expedition to Raffles, who moved to Malacca, which, as we have seen, had been taken from the Dutch in 1798, and took up his appointment as Agent to the Governor General with the Malay States. There he set up his headquarters, planning to use Malacca as the springboard for an attack on Java.

The expedition to Java set sail in June 1811, and by September the island was in British hands and Raffles was proclaimed Lieutenant Governor, subordinate to the Governor General in Calcutta. Raffles was to remain in this post until 1816 when, on instructions from the Court of Directors of the HEIC in London, he was removed from the lieutenant governorship because of the increasing cost to the Company of the administration of the island which the Court blamed on Raffles. As Victoria Glendinning states in her biography of Raffles, the whole tragedy was 'that Raffles was trying to make a first-class country out of a bankrupt one, with neither support nor investment from the Company'.[2]

As a sop, Raffles was confirmed in the post of Resident at Fort Marlborough (Bencoolen) in Sumatra and was permitted to take leave in England first, before arriving at Bencoolen in March 1818. Fort Marlborough, now the only British possession remaining in the East Indies, was quite a come-down for Raffles after the lieutenant governorship of Java. Originally established as a trading post, the huge fort was constructed in 1719 to protect English pepper traders. The Residency controlled some 300 miles (480km) of coastline around the fort, but this was, in fact, only a narrow strip of land that by 1818 was impoverished and declining in importance as a result of the fall in the price of pepper in London.

With the repossession of Malacca by the Dutch in 1818 under the Anglo-Dutch treaty of 1814 (also known as the Convention of London), the HEIC now had need of a staging post and harbour for its ships at the eastern end of the Malacca Strait. Such a staging post would prevent interference by the Dutch with the Company's China trade and ensure safe passage through the strait for HEIC ships. There can be little doubt that Raffles' ambitions were considerably greater than could be encompassed by the position of Resident at Fort Marlborough, and aware of the need to establish a base that would enable HEIC ships to pass unhindered by the Dutch into the South China Sea, and also of the fact that Penang's location could not guarantee this safe passage, he looked southwards. Believing that, strategically, the most desirable location for such a base was at or close to the narrowest part of the Malacca Strait, that is Singapore, Banka or the Riau-Lingga Islands, Raffles proposed to Calcutta that he should explore the area around the southern tip of the Malay Peninsula.

Raffles assembled a small fleet of ships at Penang in January 1819 and, together with Major William Farquhar, the resident at Malacca until its recent return to the Dutch in the previous year, sailed for the Malacca Strait to discover and establish a suitable location for the new port and trading post. Raffles had to select a spot that was not currently occupied by or under the influence of the Dutch East India Company (VOC), and he had previously considered a number of possible options. These included the island of Banka in the middle of the Malacca Strait which did not have any Dutch presence at that time, and also Bintang at the southernmost tip of Sumatra. However, it is possible, indeed most likely, that with Raffles' sense of history he had already identified the ancient port of Singapura as being the most suitable location.

The eight ships of the fleet rendezvoused at the Carimon (Karimen) Islands, which are situated some 20 miles (32km) south-west of Singapore. There a survey of the main island, Great Carimon, was carried out under the direction of Major Farquhar. Although Farquhar strongly advocated the siting of the new settlement on Great Carimon, the surveyors dismissed the two possible anchorages as being unsuitable and hardly defensible. The fleet then sailed for Singapore Island and arrived there on 28 January 1819.

The sovereignty of Singapore at this time was a complicated matter. The island was a dependency of the Sultanate of Riau, the capital of which was Bintang on the island of Sumatra and which laid claim to the Riau-Lingga islands, Singapore, and Johore and Pahang on the Malay Peninsula. When Raffles and Farquhar landed at Singapore the succession to the sultanate was currently a matter of dispute, and the government of Singapore was vested in the *Temenggong* Abdul Rahman, one of the Sultan of Riau's semi-royal Malay officials.

For over a century the Malay sultan had been only the titular head of state, as effective power in the sultanate had been wielded by the Bugis, immigrants whose leader was the *Yamtuan Muda* (Viceroy). In 1784 the Dutch drove out the *Yamtuan Muda* and installed a resident, only to

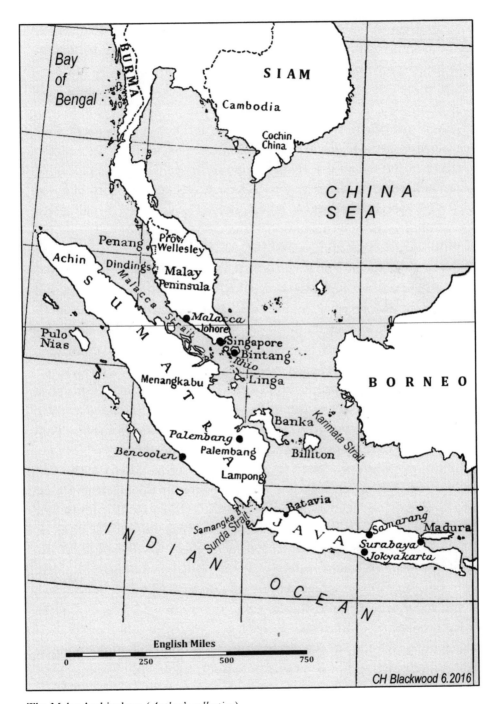

The Malay Archipelago. (*Author's collection*)

be driven out themselves by the British in 1795. The British then re-installed the *Yamtuan Muda* in Bintang. Meanwhile, the Malay sultan had established his residence on the island of Lingga, but he died in 1812 and two brothers, *Tengku* (Prince) Hussein and *Tengku* Abdul Rahman, each laid claim to the throne.

The Bugis and the Dutch supported Abdul Rahman, but Hussein had the support of two senior Malay officials, both of semi-royal descent, the *Temenggong* and the *Bendahara*. The *Temenggong* was traditionally the third highest official in the hierarchy of the sultanate, with responsibility for ports, police and markets throughout Johore, Singapore and the nearby islands, while the *Bendahara*'s fiefdom was Pahang.

With the death of the Sultan Mahmud it was incumbent upon the *Bendahara* to appoint a new sultan but, while the appointment remained disputed, *Tenku* Abdul Rahman fled to Trengganu while Hussein, the *Tengku Long* (eldest prince), remained at Riau. So when Raffles landed on Singapore Island it was with the *Temenggong* that he first had to deal. The *Tengku Long* was summoned to Singapore and on his arrival Raffles, entirely on his own authority, installed him as the Sultan of Singapore. Raffles then signed an agreement which permitted the HEIC to establish a settlement on the island, and in return a monthly allowance was to be paid to the new sultan and the *Temenggong*. So it was that Singapore was established on what can only be described as a somewhat shaky legal foundation.

Raffles left Singapore after only a few days, leaving Major Farquhar as the new Resident, and Singapore officially became a dependency of Fort Marlborough rather than Penang. However, the VOC authorities were much angered by Britain's 'annexation' of Singapore, which they considered to be within their sphere of influence. There were rumours of a Dutch attack on the new settlement, but this did not occur. Nevertheless, Raffles left detailed instructions regarding the construction of defences against such a possible attack, and these will be considered in the next chapter.

Raffles returned to Singapore for his second visit only four months after its founding, in May 1819, and found it already beginning to thrive, with a tenfold increase in the size of its population from 500 to almost 5,000 people. There was a proportionate increase, also, in trade and the shipping using the new port.

Singapore waterfront c. 1850. (*Author's collection*)

For the next three and a half years Farquhar remained as Resident, only nominally under the control of Fort Marlborough, and Raffles made his final visit to the settlement when he left Bencoolen for England in September 1822. By then Singapore had grown vastly in both size and wealth, its population having doubled in size once again since 1819, now numbering 10,000. It would seem that Raffles was most unhappy at the physical development of Singapore since his previous visit: he considered that Farquhar had disregarded his initial instructions regarding the formal town plan he had drawn up, nor had the defences Raffles had ordered been constructed. So, exercising his authority as lieutenant governor of Fort Marlborough and therefore Farquhar's superior officer, in January 1822 he recommended to the Governor General in Calcutta that Farquhar be replaced by Dr John Crawfurd of the Bengal Civil Service. Crawfurd was a colleague who had accompanied Raffles on Lord Minto's expedition to capture Java.

In April 1823, a month before the arrival of Dr Crawfurd, matters between Raffles and Farquhar came to a head and Raffles peremptorily dismissed him. Although questioning Raffles' authority to dismiss him without specific confirmation from Calcutta, Farquhar reluctantly accepted his dismissal and withdrew from Singapore, leaving Crawfurd to continue Raffles' plan for the development of the settlement.

John Crawfurd was the Resident at Singapore for three years until 1826, during which time there occurred a number of significant events that affected the settlement. In 1823 Singapore became a dependency of Bengal, and in 1824 a treaty was finally signed between Britain and the Netherlands formally settling a number of disputes. Two of the issues resolved concerned, first, the British occupation of Dutch territories captured during the recent Revolutionary and Napoleonic Wars with France and its, albeit reluctant, allies, and, second, the right to trade in the Spice Islands. Under the treaty clear spheres of influence were established by which the Dutch abandoned their claims north of the Malacca Strait in return for British recognition of Dutch rights south of the strait. As a result, Fort Marlborough at Bencoolen was ceded by the British in return for Dutch withdrawal from Malacca.

Although Crawfurd was not involved in the negotiations that led up to the signing of the Anglo–Dutch treaty he was involved in local diplomatic bargaining. On 2 August 1824 he signed a treaty with the *Temenggong* representing the Sultan which extended British control of Singapore from the small area at the mouth of the Singapore River to include the whole island.

Finally, in 1826, Singapore was removed from the authority of the Bengal Presidency, and a new colony, the Straits Settlements, was established comprising Prince of Wales Island (Penang), Singapore and Malacca, with its administrative headquarters in Georgetown on Prince of Wales Island. This new colony came directly under the Governor General in Calcutta, and in 1832 its capital was moved from Georgetown to Singapore. After the dissolution of the HEIC in 1858 the colony was administered by the Bengal Presidency until 1867, when the Straits Settlements became a Crown Colony administered by the Colonial Office in London.

The opening of the Suez Canal in 1869 and the advent of steam as a form of ship propulsion brought about an increase in British trade with the Far East and heightened Singapore's importance not only as a trading post but also as an important coaling station for the Royal Navy. Singapore was now an important strategic base and a key trading post and port of empire.

Chapter 2

The Early Fortifications: 1819–1869

The earliest fortifications of Singapore Island remain shrouded in a certain amount of mystery. On his first visit to the island, when the initial treaty was signed with the *Temenggong*, Raffles left clear orders regarding the fortification of the new settlement in his instructions to Major Farquhar:

> In determining the extent and nature of the works immediately necessary for the defence of the Port and Station my judgment has been directed in a great measure by your professional skill and experience. With this advantage, and from a careful survey of the coast by Capt. Ross, aided by my own personal inspection of the nature of the ground in the vicinity of the Settlement, I have no hesitation in conveying to you my authority for constructing the following works with the least delay practicable: on the hill overlooking the Settlement, and commanding it and a considerable portion of the anchorage, a small fort, or a commodious block-house on the principle which I have already described to you, capable of mounting eight or ten 12-pounders and of containing a magazine of brick or stone, together with a barrack for the permanent residence of 30 European Artillery and or the temporary accommodation of the rest of the garrison in case of emergency. Along the coast in the vicinity of the Settlement one or two strong batteries for the protection of the shipping and at Sandy Point [Tanjong Katong] a redoubt and to the east of it a strong battery for the same purpose. The entrenchment of the cantonment lines and a palisade as the labor [sic] can be spared from works of more immediate importance. These defences, together with a Martello tower on Deep Water Point, which it is my intention to recommend to the Supreme Government, will in my judgment render the Settlement capable of maintaining a good defence.[1]

It is difficult to establish with accuracy when the first defence works were built. Certainly, no work had yet commenced on any of the fortifications ordered by Raffles when he returned to Singapore in 1822. However, by 1824 the garrison was reported by a Dutch officer, Colonel Nahuijs, as being 'two companies of Bengalese and a detachment of 25 European Artillery', which he believed 'must hardly suffice to ensure the safety of their people and the large values which are lying in Singapore warehouses in the way of goods'.[2] The presence of European gunners certainly implies the existence of a battery or batteries between 1824 and 1834, and in the Garrison Orders there are numerous references to salutes being fired. It would seem that in 1824 the garrison included two batteries of field artillery, a heavy battery comprising five 12pdr brass guns and a 24pdr howitzer and a light battery of five 6pdr brass guns and a 12pdr howitzer.

However, there are also reports of a battery to the north of the entrance to the Singapore River which appears to have mounted six guns. This was probably the earliest battery to be built in Singapore and was essentially a temporary installation constructed of earth and sand in 1820 by Captain Henry Ralfe of the Bengal Artillery, who commanded the artillery garrison at that date. By 1827 the battery, known as Scandal Point, had fallen into decay. It was retained as a saluting battery after the construction of Fort Fullerton and was eventually abandoned in 1851, when the sea wall along the Esplanade was built.

In January 1827 Lieutenant Jackson of the Bengal Artillery was appointed Executive Officer of Public Works at Singapore, while on the same date a Captain Lake of the Madras Engineers was appointed Inspector of Stores, Works and Estimates of Prince of Wales Island, Malacca and Singapore.[3] At this date the garrison included, in addition to the European gunners, a number of Golundauz, native soldiers of the European-officered artillery battalion.

Lieutenant Jackson drew a map of Singapore that was published in London in June 1828 showing a battery on the point overlooking the entrance to the Singapore River, with a second battery position a little further north on the edge of the sea. Until recently this map has been taken to be an accurate representation of the new settlement at that date, but the current view is that it is, in fact, Lieutenant Jackson's proposed plan for the settlement rather

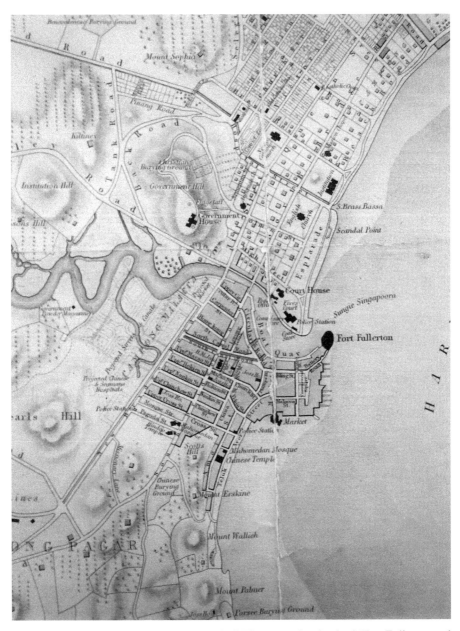

Map of Singapore Town 1844 by John Turnbull Thomson, showing both Fort Fullerton and the Battery at Scandal Point. (*Author's collection*)

than a true picture of the position then. Interestingly, the battery north of the river is not shown on Coleman's map of 1836; the site of the battery is shown but not noted as such on Thomson's map of 1844.

It would seem that work on the defences proceeded at a leisurely pace. The first work of fortification to be built appears to have been the small battery at Scandal Point. This battery is referred to by Captain Lake who, on a false report of the outbreak of war between England and France and Spain having been received in Calcutta, was sent from Penang to report on the fortifications required to provide an adequate defence for Singapore.

In his inventory of the scanty defensive works existing at the time of his report Captain Lake detailed a magazine in a masonry building with an arched bomb-proof roof and a line of fortification, and a battery made entirely of earth. Although he gave no indication of the number of guns mounted in the battery, it appears there were probably six. He reported that the temporary battery had fallen into decay and that all the gun carriages were quite rotten and unserviceable.[4]

Lake inspected the environs of the settlement only to discover that certain areas that were important for the siting of a covered way and glacis had already been built over by some of the more prominent citizens, so that the expense involved in acquiring the land would be great. Taking this fact into consideration, he looked at how the settlement could be protected from attack from the sea or bombardment by enemy naval vessels.

In order to achieve this aim Lake drew up a somewhat elaborate plan of fortifications which included defences to secure the harbour, a line of batteries between St George's Island (Pulau Blakang Mati) and Sandy Point (Tanjong Katong), and a fortified post for the defence of the garrison in a last resort. For the defence of the harbour he proposed a casemated redoubt mounting twenty-seven heavy guns situated on the southern point of the entrance to the Singapore River, a location which he had ordered to be cleared 'for the purpose of laying a platform battery'.[5] The redoubt was to be separated from the town by a ditch and drawbridge and was to be defensible against musketry or escalade but not against artillery fire. In addition, he planned to support the redoubt by means of a half-moon battery mounting seven heavy guns. This work was to be named Prince's, or possibly Princess, Battery, and there seems to be doubt as to whether it was ever built.

To protect the coastline from St George's Island to Sandy Point Lake planned a line of four batteries extending from Palmer's Hill on the southeast point of the island to Sandy Point to the north of the settlement. Three of these batteries were to be open works, that is to say not casemated or closed at the gorge, while the fourth, at Sandy Point, was to be casemated and similar to the redoubt to be built for the defence of the harbour. Lake's reasoning was that the battery at Sandy Point would be isolated and, if it were an open battery, might be easily captured and its guns turned to fire on the settlement.

Finally, the matter of a position on which to build a fortified post for 'the protection of public stores and treasure and to a certain extent that of individuals, and to form a defensive point of general rendezvous in the event of an enemy effecting a landing' needed to be selected.[6] Ideally, such a post should be sited where it could support the other batteries and engage any enemy ship that might enter the harbour. However, this all proved impossible to achieve due to the manner in which the settlement had developed. Instead, Lake found that only two locations seemed possible, but both had a number of disadvantages.

The two locations were Government or Residency Hill, on which Major Farquhar's house had been built, and Captain Pearl's Hill, or simply Pearl's Hill, named after a prominent Singapore resident, Captain James Pearl, owner and captain of the merchantman *Indiana*. Government Hill was the higher of the two and the larger, but required fortification works of considerable extent and a large garrison to defend them. Pearl's Hill, on the other hand, though lower in height, was considered by Lake to be of a more convenient size, so requiring a smaller garrison. In addition, there was the advantage that its guns would be able to fire into New Harbour, the stretch of water between the main island and Blakang Mati. Lake recommended that the fortified post for the defence of the garrison should be built, initially as an earthwork, on Pearl's Hill.

The recommendations in Captain Lake's report were never implemented. Although work had commenced on Lake's scheme of fortification, orders came from the newly-appointed Governor General in Calcutta, Lieutenant General Lord William Bentinck, that work should stop. Bentinck was engaged in an extensive range of cost-cutting measures in order to improve the financial position of the HEIC, and these included the cancellation of the new works of fortification for Singapore.

Lake and his family perished when, on their return voyage to England in 1830, the vessel in which they were sailing sank without trace somewhere in the Indian Ocean, and his plans sank with him. The works of fortification that were completed were the redoubt on the southern point of the mouth of the Singapore River, referred to in later maps as Battery Point, and the half-moon battery that supported it. The redoubt contained an artillery barracks and officers' quarters and was named Fort Fullerton in honour of Robert Fullerton, who became the first Governor of the Straits Settlements in 1826.

Captain Lake's was to be only the first of a number of such reports on the defences of Singapore between 1827 and 1869. In 1843 a new Governor of the Straits Settlements, Colonel William Butterworth, was appointed, who was the first military officer to hold the appointment since Major Farquhar was the Resident at Singapore. Butterworth's appointment meant, naturally, an increased interest in defence matters, and it seems likely that he requested Captain Lake's plans for the defences, since shortly after taking up his post he was informed by the Madras government that Lake's plans had been lost.[7] The Madras government then dispatched Captain Samuel Best, Madras Engineers, to draw up new fortification plans.

Best arrived in Singapore in 1844 with instructions 'to report upon the particular works which may be required for the defence of that island under such instructions as he may receive from the Supreme Government'.[8] He endorsed most of the proposals made in Lake's earlier report and had, in November 1843, already produced a plan for a fort to be built at the mouth of the Singapore River. The rebuilt Fort Fullerton was to be horseshoe-shaped with a small wet ditch on the landward side, and included accommodation for the artillery officers and barrack accommodation for the gun lascars. The fort was to have been armed with some thirty guns, mounted on two levels, firing *en barbette* and in casemates through embrasures. However, when finally constructed, Fort Fullerton was armed with a smaller number of heavy guns.

Best did not agree that Pearl's Hill was the most suitable position for the fortified post designed as a keep of last resort. Instead, he recommended another hill, Mount Wallich, a feature closer to the seashore, to be supported by an infantry redoubt on Pearl's Hill.

As well as concluding that the line of batteries proposed by Lake for the defence of the shoreline were properly sited, Best recommended five further batteries to protect the New Harbour. Two of these were to be sited on St George's Island (Blakang Mati), one on Mount Serapong on the eastern end of the island and the other on Mount Siloso at its north-western tip. The other proposed positions for batteries were on the islands of Pulau Brani and Pulau Hantu and at Berlayer Point on the southern shore of the main island. All three were to be sited in order to cover with fire the narrow western entrance to the New Harbour. With the exception of the position on Pulau Hantu, the sites selected by Best for batteries for the defence of the New Harbour, although not built at this date, would subsequently feature in all later plans for the defence of Singapore.

The very dilatory approach to the fortification of Singapore on the part of the Supreme Government of the HEIC was probably due to the absence of any obvious external threat at this time, as well as to the general policy of reliance upon the Royal Navy and the marine forces of the HEIC to defend the Straits Settlements. Nevertheless, Major General Sir George Pollock, the Military Member of the Council of India, appears to have been sufficiently worried about the island's defences to express his grave concern. In May 1845 he described the existing defences as being a half-sunken battery for six guns that lacked the range to fire on hostile ships – a reference, it is assumed, to the battery at Scandal Point.[9]

In 1851 the subject of a review of the Singapore defences arose once again. The Governor General was of the opinion that 'The defences of the settlements [Singapore, Penang and Malacca] should be calculated only for the repulse of privateering attacks, or for resistance against assault in the temporary absence of men-of-war and steamers from the port.' He then instructed that 'The defences should be limited to two Batteries of four heavy guns each, with one similar Battery for the Back Bay [New Harbour] if it shall be considered absolutely necessary.'[10]

Once again, little action was taken with regard to Captain Best's report, and it was to be ten years before the subject once again came to the attention of the Indian government, although in 1851 a small improvement was made with the dispatch of eight 8in SB shell guns to replace the guns in Fort Fullerton and the battery at Scandal Point.

An increase in piracy and fear of internal unrest amongst the population led the HEIC government to authorize the construction of two additional batteries in the following year. However, the Governor, Colonel Butterworth, questioned the siting of the new batteries and asked for a military engineer to be sent to Singapore to report on the sites for the two batteries and on the island's defences generally.

The officer sent in 1853 was Captain Henry Yule, Bengal Engineers, who in 1855 was to accompany Sir Arthur Phayre's mission to the Kingdom of Ava [Burma] and later wrote the acclaimed book *A Narrative of the Mission to the Court of Ava*, published in 1858. Yule's report recommended changes in the sites originally selected for the two batteries previously authorized. The report was approved the following year, when Britain and France were engaged in the Crimean War against Russia. He also recommended changes to the existing Fort Fullerton and the construction of a battery and tower between Sandy Point and Tanjong Katong; but these were not proceeded with because of doubts concerning the feasibility of constructing them on what was described as shifting sand. Governor Blundell also believed that the Sandy Point fortification would be situated too far from support by the garrison in the town.

The sites for the two new batteries were on the lower slopes of Mount Palmer and on the forward slope of Mount Faber. In addition, Yule recommended a battery of two 13in SB mortars on the summit of Mount Faber; these two mortars were the only weapons able to fire into New Harbour at this time.

The installation on the lower slopes of Mount Palmer was given the name Lake's Battery and was designed to mount six heavy guns. Although the Inspector-General of Ordnance and Magazines considered the 56pdr 98cwt SB gun to be in every respect an efficient if not better piece of ordnance than the 68pdr 95cwt SB gun, the latter were to be issued in Singapore in future, as the 56pdr guns were 'following [sic] into disuse' at Woolwich and it was considered important 'to maintain a single calibre in the batteries'.[11] The armament of the two batteries at this time was:

Fort Fullerton	3 x 56pdr 98cwt SB guns
	2 x 32pdr 63cwt SB guns
Mount Faber Battery	2 x 56pdr 98cwt SB guns

The estimated cost of the changes to Fort Fullerton and the construction of Lake's Battery on Mount Palmer came to Rs14,860 (£3,935), but the actual cost amounted to only Rs159 (£42). In the words of a memorandum from a senior HEIC clerk:

> Government expressed its satisfaction at the manner in which the defences of Singapore have been completed by convict labour under Captain H. Man, 49th MNI, Executive Officer and Superintendent of Convicts and Roads at Singapore. The work was executed with a saving of Rs14,701 (£3,895) consequent on the work having been entirely performed by convict labour.[12]

Despite the recommendations of both Captain Lake and Captain Best, the proposal to build a defensive post or place of refuge for the garrison in Singapore remained in abeyance. However, in 1854 serious rioting had broken out in what was now the substantial town of Singapore between two groups of its Chinese inhabitants, the Hokkien and the Teochew, and this concentrated the minds of the Governor and his advisors regarding protection for the European population from civil unrest. In April 1856 Governor Blundell wrote to the Secretary to the Government of India at Fort William in Calcutta and expressly pressed for the construction of a place of refuge for the white population, the European artillerymen and soldiers of the garrison, government officials and merchants and their families, to protect them from attack by the indigenous population. The site for such a place of refuge suggested by the governor was Pearl's Hill rather than Government Hill or Mount Wallich, the former still considered to be too large to be easily defended and the latter too small.

The conventional military solution to the problem of defending a small colonial population at this time was to construct a citadel, as had been done on the islands of St Helena and Mauritius, usually on a hill or other prominent feature. In 1856 this is what the Calcutta government authorized to be built. Governor Blundell recited the advantages of Pearl's Hill and the disadvantages of Government Hill as possible sites for a position of refuge. He considered Pearl's Hill to have ample space for the barracks, arsenal and commissariat stores, while being close to the military cantonment. It also had command over the town. On the other hand, Government Hill, in the Governor's view, lacked space, particularly as Government House was sited there, and it was further away from the military cantonment. The Governor also recommended that two gunboats should be sent to Singapore, with the dual role of defending the colony and dealing with pirates.

Captain Yule, when consulted, agreed with the proposal for a citadel and supported the Governor's view that Pearl's Hill was the most suitable site. In August 1856, therefore, the Governor General authorized the construction of a fort subject to the approval of estimates and plans to be submitted by the Singapore authorities.[13]

Governor Blundell forwarded a rough plan of the fortification to be built on Pearl's Hill, and initial preparatory work was undertaken on the construction of a small fort. However, on receipt of the sketch plan which was accompanied by estimates for barracks and other buildings, the Governor General in Council refused to approve the design submitted. This initial refusal probably resulted from a period of retrenchment and reorganization in the Indian Public Works department and a shortage of convict labour in the Straits Settlements. The Indian government informed the Governor that fully professional plans and estimates of costs were required and insisted on dispatching an engineer officer to Singapore. The officer selected was Captain George Collyer, Madras Engineers, who was appointed to the post of Chief Engineer of the Public Works Department in the Straits Settlements.

The outbreak of the Indian Mutiny in 1857 added to the pressure for a secure refuge for the European population of Singapore, and in December of that year Captain Collyer submitted his 'Report on the Works proposed to be erected on Pearl's Hill as a citadel or strong place of refuge and defence against internal Aggression'.[14] The proposal, which included plans for a citadel, barracks, an arsenal and a commissariat building, was forwarded by the Governor to Calcutta in February 1858. Collyer, though, was now having second thoughts about the choice of Pearl's Hill for this complex of buildings, feeling that there was insufficient space on the hill to hold them all.

The lack of space on Pearl's Hill was probably the main reason for a brief flirtation with a proposal to build a 'Maximilian' tower there rather than a citadel. The 'Maximilian' was a very large gun tower designed, originally, by Prince Maximilian-Neuwied and much favoured by Austrian engineers, who built a number to defend Linz.[15] The tower was surrounded by a ditch and glacis, and ten or eleven heavy guns were mounted on a gun platform on top of the tower, so a structure of this type was also expensive to build.

Collyer now returned to the idea of using Government Hill as the site of the citadel, particularly as he was of the belief that Singapore should be effectively defended against foreign aggression as well as internal unrest. When forwarding his plans and estimates for a fortification on Pearl's Hill he commenced his covering letter by saying:

> Had he not been fettered by the orders of Government he would not have chosen Pearl's Hill as the site for the works but Government Hill and the adjacent hill called Mount Sophia. Government Hill is the natural key of the place which with the adjacent height is spacious enough to contain all the required buildings; it commands the dangerous part of the Town completely; it is easier of access as a place of refuge for the European Community; and if suitably fortified it could be made to form an important feature in the sea defences of the place.[16]

He therefore recommended to Governor Blundell that Government Hill should be selected as the location for the citadel. His argument was that it could both act as a refuge and mount guns that could defend the harbour, since it commanded the town and had space for a battery of 68pdr guns at the south end.

Governor Blundell was stunned by Collyer's elaborate plans for Government Hill and still held to the view that Pearl's Hill was the most appropriate site for the citadel, believing that only a simple place of refuge was required. He warned the government in Calcutta that the cost of fortifying Government Hill would be prohibitive, converting Singapore into a military fortress which he believed to be incompatible with its role as a free port. Calcutta was gradually changing its view, however, concerning the defences of Singapore. There was now a feeling in government circles that the Singapore defences should, indeed, be capable of resisting attack by foreign aggressors as well as civil unrest, so the Pearl's Hill site was rejected and Captain Collyer was ordered to forward new proposals.

In June 1858 Collyer sent new proposals to Calcutta headed 'Report on the Land Defences of Singapore'. He proposed siting the citadel on Government Hill, as Captain Charles Faber, the Superintending Engineer of Public Works of the Straits Settlements, had proposed in 1846. In addition, to support the citadel on Government Hill Collyer planned batteries on Mount Sophia and Institution Hill, both situated to the rear of Government Hill.

Collyer followed his first report very quickly with a second, 'On the Sea Coast Defences of Singapore', the aim of which was to secure the town against bombardment and to ensure the protection of New Harbour.[17] He first reviewed the existing defences, which he considered to be quite

An 8in shell gun at Fort Denison in Sydney Harbour, similar to the 8in guns mounted within Fort Canning. (*Author's photograph*)

inadequate. He believed the batteries on Mount Faber and Mount Palmer and in Fort Fullerton to be altogether insufficient for the task of protecting the town and anchorage. Captain Collyer described Fort Fullerton as having earthen parapets faced with bricks and having no furnace or expense magazines (small magazines containing ammunition for immediate use); he considered that it should be completely remodelled. His recommendations for the fort included rearming it with seven 68pdr 95cwt SB guns, two 8in (203mm) 65cwt SB shell guns and two 8in SB howitzers.

New batteries were proposed for Sandy Point (Tanjong Katong), consisting of ten 68pdr 95cwt SB guns and three 8in 65cwt SB shell guns. There was also to be a battery overlooking Kampong Glam. A new battery was planned for Mount Palmer of four 68pdr guns, one 8in 65cwt SB shell gun and two 13in (330mm) SB mortars. Collyer also recommended that a new site be found for the old Lake's Battery. The report then considered the new works required to defend New Harbour and for this Collyer suggested

The 68pdr 95 cwt gun, one of the most powerful guns of its time, was introduced into service in 1846. The photograph shows one of these guns outside the National Army Museum in London. (*Author's photograph*)

batteries on Pagar Point at the foot of Mount Palmer and on Pulau Brani, and two batteries on Blakang Mati, one at Mount Serapong and the other at Rimau Point.

There is no doubt that when officers of the Royal Engineers (and that includes engineer officers of the HEIC and Indian armies) were asked to plan the defences of a location they could seldom resist the temptation to plan the most sophisticated and expensive schemes possible. So, perhaps, it is not surprising that Governor Blundell opposed the concept of the large-scale fortification of Singapore proposed by Captain Collyer, on the grounds of expense if for no other reason. Blundell still believed that, ultimately, the security of the town lay in the ships of the Royal Navy – which was also the cheapest option! However, the governor did authorize work to start on the citadel and on the reconstruction of Fort Fullerton at a cost of some Rs93,250 (£24,700), and he instructed that all batteries should be enclosed at the rear.

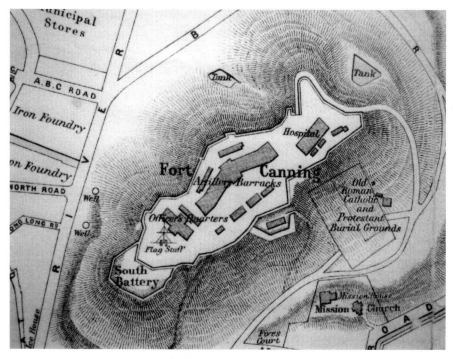

Plan of Fort Canning in 1878. (TNA WO 78/2420)

By May 1859 seven 68pdr 95cwt SB guns and two 13in SB mortars had been mounted in field works at the south end of Government Hill, and the following year work had been completed on the expense magazine, the gun platforms and a 'making-up' room at the South Battery, as well as a postern gate, scarp and counterscarp. By September 1860 the top of Government Hill had been surrounded by a parapet 14ft (4m) thick, and beyond the parapet the fort had a steep earthen bank 20ft (6.5m) high, then a dry ditch 6ft (2m) wide and then another bank of earth 6ft (2m) high. The fort had one main entrance on the north side, and the gate itself was in the form of a miniature citadel, with an internal staircase leading to a flat roof surrounded by a loopholed parapet.

The citadel was completed in 1861, the walls forming an irregular outline following the natural configuration of the hill. It consisted of two parts, the main fort and the South Battery, the latter situated 30ft (8.5m) below the level of the main fort with its gorge closed by the parapet wall of the fort;

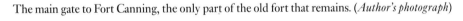

The main gate to Fort Canning, the only part of the old fort that remains. (*Author's photograph*)

communication between the two was by means of a flight of steps. The main fort had a semi-subterranean magazine that could contain 2,500 barrels of gunpowder, six expense magazines, barrack accommodation for two garrison companies of artillery, a canteen, a plunge bath (swimming pool), skittle alley, schoolroom and library. There were also officers' quarters for two captains and four subalterns, and stabling for horses. In 1867 the buildings were all lit by gas lamps.

By 1861 the merchants of Singapore had begun to oppose loudly the cost of the military works and the garrison. The whole of the Public Works budget for the Straits Settlements in the fiscal year 1861/62 was earmarked for constructing barracks for European troops and repairing and completing military works already authorized. To exacerbate the discontent, Captain Collyer had monopolized the convict labour force for the citadel on Government Hill, named Fort Canning after the then Governor General, and as a result all other public works in Singapore had come to a standstill. At the same time, discussions were taking place concerning the transfer of the Straits Settlements from the Government of India to the British government as a Crown Colony, and the cost of the military garrison was an important, and difficult, aspect of the transfer. In 1861 the Secretary of State for India ordered a stop to all military construction work in Singapore until the transfer question was settled.

By 1861 the existing defences of Singapore were:

Fort Canning	8 x 8in SB shell guns
Fort Canning South Battery	7 x 68pdr 95cwt SB guns
	2 x 13in SB mortars
Fort Fullerton	7 x 68pdr 95cwt SB guns
	1 x 13in SB mortar
Mount Palmer Battery	5 x 56pdr 98cwt SB guns
Mount Faber Battery	2 x 56pdr 98cwt SB guns
Mount Faber Mortar Battery	2 x 13in SB mortars

However, there was a considerable shortage of gunners to man these pieces, with only forty-seven European artillerymen and twenty-one Ordnance lascars on the strength of the garrison. This seems to imply that the Indian government still regarded Singapore as a relatively low priority when it came to men and money.

The state of the fortifications in 1864 can probably be best described by John Cameron FRGS, who visited Singapore in that year and the following year published *Our Tropical Possessions in Malayan India*. He described a visit to the batteries on Mount Faber as follows:

> On top of this hill [Mount Faber] are two mortars, and lower down is a battery of two 56-pounder guns, with barracks attached, forming part of the far-famed fortifications of Singapore. It is difficult to say whether the two gaping mortars on the top of the hill, or the two lonely guns below convey the greatest feeling of desolation and decay. The very sepoys that guard the latter – for they don't man them – seem touched with the melancholy of neglect.[18]

It should also be said that Cameron noted, presciently, that not a single heavy gun mounted on any of the forts was capable of being turned to direct its fire inland.

In 1867 the decision was duly taken to remove the government of the Straits Settlements from Calcutta, and the Straits Settlements became a Crown Colony administered by the Colonial Office in London. During the 1840s and 1850s, as Singapore's prosperity increased, a movement to oppose control by the HEIC had grown steadily, culminating in a virulent newspaper campaign in the mid-1850s. The inhabitants of Singapore suspected that the HEIC regarded Singapore as a useful source of revenue and they protested strongly against any attempt to remove the town's free port status. As a result, the Imperial government declared itself in favour of the transfer of Singapore to Imperial rule in 1858, some nine years before such rule became effective.

Three years earlier, in 1864, the governor of Hong Kong, Sir Hercules Robinson, was requested by the Duke of Newcastle, the Secretary of State for the Colonies, to report on the military defence of the Straits Settlements before their transfer to Imperial rule. He was to chair a committee that included Colonel Orfeur Cavenagh, then governor of the Straits Settlements, and a senior engineer officer, Colonel James Freeth RE. The committee reviewed the existing defences and came to the conclusion that while the western approaches to New Harbour were reasonably secure, the eastern entrance was undefended. They also accepted the view of the governor and other senior citizens that Fort Fullerton was actually useless as a work of defence. With the development of Singapore, the fort was now in the commercial heart of the town and, as a battery *à fleur d'eau*, that is sited on the shoreline with its embrasures only 15ft (4.6m) above sea level, shipping in the harbour would mask the fire of the fort's guns which, in themselves, would attract enemy fire on to the town.

The batteries on Mount Palmer and Mount Faber were considered to be adequate, despite John Cameron's somewhat disparaging view of Mount Faber, with both having expense magazines and guardhouses. The Mount Faber battery was described as having been completed in 1861 at a cost of Rs3,775 (£1,000), while the battery on Mount Palmer had cost double that amount. Both batteries were still armed with 56pdr guns rather than the more powerful 68pdrs. However, both batteries, together with Fort Fullerton and Fort Canning, were considered to be adequate for the defence of the town and the harbour. The threat level was considered to be if 'one or possibly two hostile cruisers should such escape the vigilance of our Squadrons, and visit the Port during the temporary absence of any of our Naval Forces'.[19]

The fortification at Tanjong Katong, which the committee proposed should be built to defend the eastern entrance to New Harbour, was to be a substantial work. It was to mount ten heavy guns and its cost, including a bomb-proof barrack, was estimated at Rs30,000 (£8,000). However, the committee believed that much of the cost could be defrayed by the sale of Fort Fullerton. A fort on Tanjong Katong, or Sandy Point as it had previously been known, had long been mooted, but despite the views of the committee the Tanjong Katong fort remained just a proposal. Nevertheless, in 1865 work commenced on dismantling Fort Fullerton, but the batteries which had been recommended for Pagar Point, Pulau Brani and Blakang Mati did not materialize.

Now that the Straits Settlements were a Crown Colony, the Imperial government in London began to look closely at the colony's military expenditure, with a view to setting a contribution to be paid by the colony. By 1863 almost half of Singapore's local revenue went on military expenditure, and this produced considerable disenchantment amongst the merchants and traders of Singapore.

There was strong public feeling in the colony that the new, and expensive, fortifications proposed for its defence were more for the benefit of the British government than for the inhabitants of the colony. Negotiations over the controversial issue of the colony's financial contribution towards the costs of the garrison and defences extended over a period of some three years, and eventually agreement was reached. The colony's contribution was set at £59,300 annually, but by means of a rather odd accounting arrangement the Imperial government was to receive £50,000 annually, while the balance of £9,300 was to be retained by the colony to be used as the local authorities saw fit.

In 1867, at the time of the transfer of the control of the Straits Settlements to the Colonial Office, the garrison of Singapore comprised two European batteries of artillery and two regiments of Madras Native Infantry. The Robinson committee recommended that since the garrison was essentially required simply to quell any internal disturbances it could be safely reduced to two batteries of European gunners and six companies of the recently formed Ceylon Rifle Regiment, a body originally recruited by the Dutch mainly from the indigenous Malay population.

In 1868 the infantry garrison was reduced when one of the Madras Native Infantry regiments was withdrawn; the War Office in London, with an eye to the strategic position of Singapore, then proposed to station a wing (half a battalion) of a European regiment in the colony to act as a small strategic reserve for the area, including Hong Kong. However, the War Office was told in no uncertain terms by the colony's government that the stationing of these troops in Singapore was for the convenience of the War Office and should cause no additional expense to the colony. The proposal was subsequently dropped when it was discovered that the barrack accommodation at Tanglin was not suitable for European troops.

It soon became clear, however, that despite the reduction in the strength of the garrison the contribution made by the Imperial government would fall well short of the total defence expenditure in the colony. Before the matter could be debated further, however, the situation would change as advances in military technology and in the British government's approach to the financing of its colonies' defence requirements brought about a complete reappraisal of Singapore's defences.

Chapter 3

A Time of Change: 1865–1890

T he middle years of the nineteenth century were a period of great technological change, not least in the matter of armaments and ships. Developments in the use of steam power and improvements in metallurgical techniques, in firstly iron and then steel, contributed to revolutionary changes in the construction of warships, guns and, ultimately, coastal defence forts and batteries.

The Warships

The design of warships did not change materially between the middle of the seventeenth century and the accession of Queen Victoria in 1837. For nearly two hundred years the sailing line-of-battle ship armed with broadside batteries of smooth-bore cannon was the supreme arbiter of naval warfare. However, with the advent of the steam engine in the early years of the nineteenth century and its application to ship propulsion it became apparent that the supremacy of the sailing warship was soon to be challenged. Although steam power was first used in commercial shipping, it was not long before the navies of the world began to use it as an adjunct to sail. The Royal Navy was initially suspicious of the concept: the new engines were inefficient, they needed large amounts of coal, and the means of propulsion, paddle wheels in large boxes on each side of the ship, were obviously very vulnerable to gunfire.

By the 1840s some small steam paddle warships were in service with the Royal Navy. These were classed as 'steam corvettes' and by 1860 had seen action in Burma and China. However, it was the invention of the screw propeller in 1837, together with an improvement in the efficiency of marine steam engines, that ensured the adoption of steam power by the Royal Navy for major warships. Initially, steam was used as an auxiliary form of propulsion in older sailing line-of-battleships, which were refitted; new screw battleships were also built, though still with sail as their primary form of propulsion.

Prior to 1858 all the battleships in the Royal Navy were wooden-hulled, but during the Crimean War the French made use of a number of iron-plated floating batteries, which proved to be very successful since they were virtually invulnerable to the fire of the Russian shore batteries armed with smooth-bore guns. This apparent invulnerability was not lost on the French navy, and in 1859 they laid down the hull of the first ironclad warship, *La Gloire*, which was followed by three more ships of the same class. Although these were only clad with iron over a wooden hull, at a stroke the French navy had overtaken the Royal Navy. In the words of a French naval officer at the time, '[France] has command of the Channel at the present moment.'

The British wasted not a moment in designing and building their answer to *La Gloire* and her sister ships. In 1860 HMS *Warrior*, the first warship in the world to be built entirely of iron and with additional armour, was

HMS *Warrior*. The restored warship is preserved as a museum ship at Portsmouth. (*Author's photograph*)

launched. This ship and her sister ship HMS *Black Prince* had an armoured belt of iron 4.5in (11mm) thick, backed by a further 18in (457mm) of teak. When completed, these two ships were the largest and most powerful in any navy at that time. Both were steam-propelled and had a top speed of fourteen knots.

HMS *Warrior* and HMS *Black Prince* revolutionized naval tactics as they were fast, no longer reliant upon the wind and heavily armed, though there was still the drawback that they lacked endurance when using steam power alone. As a result, the importance of many British colonial possessions was greatly increased because of their value as coaling stations.

The American Civil War (1861–5) saw the further development of ironclad warships: the United States Navy used vessels they termed 'monitors', and these provided practical evidence of the effectiveness of naval armour against solid shot and shells fired by smooth-bore guns. Suddenly ships had become invulnerable to the fire of coastal artillery, and the introduction of armoured turrets on these ships enabled their largest calibre gun to be mounted and fired almost independently of the direction of the ship.

The monitors were essentially coastal defence ships, powered only by steam and with a low freeboard and poor sea-going qualities. A number of these vessels were built for the Royal Navy and colonial navies, including HMVS *Cerberus* for the defence of Melbourne harbour, and two were ordered by the India Office for the defence of Bombay. The latter, HMS *Magdala* and HMS *Abyssinia*, were each completed in 1870. HMS *Magdala* was a sister ship to HMVS *Cerberus*, with a speed of 10.5 knots and an armament of four 10in (250mm) RML guns in two turrets. HMS *Abyssinia* was smaller due to financial constraints, with a displacement of 2,300 tons, but was otherwise similar in design and had a speed of 9.5 knots. HMS *Magdala* cost £132,400 to build; HMS *Abyssinia* was cheaper at £116,549.

However, for the next twenty years most major warships other than the monitors retained sail as an auxiliary form of propulsion – until the completion of HMS *Devastation* for the Royal Navy in 1873. This ship dispensed with masts for sails and was armed with four 12in (300mm) RML guns in two armoured turrets. She proved successful in trials, being a steady gun platform and a good steamer, and was followed six years later by HMS *Dreadnought*, another turret ship designed without auxiliary sail.

HMS *Devastation* was the first ocean-going battleship not to be equipped with sails. It was a mastless turret ship and the forerunner of the capital ships of the twentieth century. (*Author's collection*)

A further development that affected ship design at this time was the development of the Whitehead torpedo; this brought into being a new type of vessel built to carry these weapons and known as a 'torpedo boat'. Initially very small, of no more than 20 tons displacement, these were fast, with speeds approaching 20 knots, but lightly armed. It was these vessels and their larger successors, the torpedo boat destroyers, that led to the development of the quick-firing (QF) gun, since the rates of fire of the muzzle-loading and early breech-loading (BL) guns were too slow to ensure hits on such fleeting targets.

The years from 1875 to 1895 were a period of experiment in ship design for the Royal Navy. It struggled to combine effectively steam propulsion, weight of armour and fuel capacity in the design of its new ships, while at the same time endeavouring to solve the problem of arming these ships with suitable guns. Rifled muzzle-loading (RML) guns were no longer suited to naval use, because in order to penetrate the increasing thickness of armour used on foreign warships the guns had to be made ever larger. However, any attempt to increase their barrel length was restricted by the problem of loading the gun. In the larger battleships this was partially overcome by lowering the barrel muzzle to deck level and loading the gun hydraulically through an aperture in the deck in front of the turret. However, this meant that loading became slower and was also potentially dangerous, because there was always the possibility of loading a second charge and shell on top of a misfire, as happened in HMS *Thunderer* in 1879, causing an explosion which killed eleven men.

All this brought about the introduction of large calibre breech-loading guns, now possible because of the invention of an improved breech mechanism. At first, these guns were set in open *barbette* mountings, but subsequently armoured turrets were introduced. This new armament included the very largest 12in (304mm) and 13.5in (342mm) guns, and even an enormous, but unsuccessful, 16.25in (412mm) gun, as well as smaller quick-firing guns using fixed case ammunition.

So by the last quarter of the nineteenth century there had been startling advances in the construction of warships and their armament. These advances meant that all existing coastal defence forts and batteries were now obsolete, and new methods of construction became necessary to provide adequate protection against the threat of large high-explosive shells fired with improved accuracy, thanks to the introduction of rifled barrels, from greater distances offshore.

The Guns

The first major improvement to the smooth-bore weapon which had been the main armament of all the world's armies and navies for the past three centuries was the development of the shell gun. Prior to the 1820s smooth-bore guns fired mainly solid shot, sometimes heated to red heat for use against wooden ships, as well as canister and grapeshot for use against personnel. The only explosive shells were those fired from high-angle mortars and howitzers. However, in the 1820s a French officer, Colonel Paixhans, developed a method of firing explosive shells from large guns. These shells, although not possessing the penetrative power of solid shot, could cause damage to wooden ships by wrecking their rigging and causing fires to break out.

The Paixhans gun was demonstrated in 1821, but it took almost fifteen years before the French finally adopted it for general use. The British quickly followed suit, in 1841 developing the 8in (203mm) and 10in (254mm) SB shell guns primarily for use aboard warships. In addition, there was a new 56pdr smooth-bore gun, but this was 11ft (3.38m) long, weighed 98cwt and was considered only suitable 'to the Salients of Coast Batteries and to Cavaliers or heights of the Sea Defences of Fortresses, to be always mounted *en barbette* on ground platforms'.[1] The 56pdr gun and the 10in SB shell gun were not used in any great numbers by the Army, and it was the smaller and lighter 8in gun that was preferred both by the Royal Navy and the Army. The 8in gun was 6ft 8in (2.05m) long, weighed 50cwt (2,500kg) and could be mounted on a standard pattern traversing platform. The gun was easier to handle than the 56pdr, and this was a great advantage since it reduced the size of the gun crew.

Even as these guns and the heavier 68pdr SB gun were entering service, experiments were being carried out using guns with rifled barrels. By rifling the barrel of the gun a greater muzzle velocity could be obtained, and this resulted in increased penetration of the new cast iron armour that was gradually being introduced by the navies of Europe and America. A number of artillery experts had been attempting to develop an effective rifled gun. Mr C.W. Lancaster had rifled the barrels of a number of 68pdr SB cast iron guns according to his own principle, and these were used at the siege of Sebastopol in the Crimean War. However, with an oval barrel and a twist in the bore these guns frequently experienced problems when projectiles jammed in the bore, and they were very unpopular with gunners.

In France the Emperor Napoleon III, a noted expert on artillery matters, continued experimenting with rifled guns after the end of the Crimean War. Under his direction the French army developed a simpler form of rifling comprising six shallow grooves into which fitted two bands of studs projecting from the cylindrical shell. A number of guns using this form of rifling were used in Algeria with considerable success, and this experience persuaded the French army to adopt rifled guns in place of smooth-bores.

In Britain a number of manufacturers were experimenting with rifling, including William Armstrong, Joseph Whitworth and Alexander Blakely. These experiments were combined with research into the manufacture of guns using different materials. Traditionally, artillery pieces had been made of either bronze or cast iron, the former being expensive and the latter deficient in tensile strength so restricting the size of the gunpowder charge that could be used. In the middle of the nineteenth century steel was still not a dependable material, so the gun makers increasingly turned to wrought iron.

All three British manufacturers, Armstrong, Whitworth and Blakely, also experimented with the method of manufacture: instead of boring guns out from a solid lump of iron they each developed a stronger wrought iron gun which, in the case of Armstrong's and Blakely's, was built up by means of heating and shrinking a number of wrought iron tubes one upon another in order to increase the gun's strength. Whitworth's method differed in that the cylindrical wrought iron tubes were forced over each other by hydraulic pressure rather than by heating and shrinking.

While these developments were taking place in manufacturing, William Armstrong was also engaged in the construction of an effective breech-loading gun. For centuries all large artillery pieces had been loaded through the muzzle because of the problem of preventing the escape of gas from a breech-loading gun. In 1856 Armstrong developed a rifled breech-loading (RBL) gun with a block acting as a plug placed in the breech of the gun and screwed up against the end of the barrel by means of a hollow screw. The projectile and charge were loaded through the bored-out breech screw, and the vent piece, which acted as a wedge and was also bored out to allow ignition of the charge, was dropped into place and held tight by the breech screw. The gun used a special shell that was coated with lead and made slightly larger than the bore. On firing the lead coating acted as a gas seal and driving band.

The Armstrong system of gun construction was adopted by both the Royal Navy and the British Army, and Armstrong donated his patents to the government in return for a knighthood and the position of Engineer of Rifled Ordnance to the War Department. His rival Blakely hotly disputed Armstrong's right to the patents, protesting that Armstrong had pirated his original designs. There would appear to be evidence to support Blakely's claim, but it would seem that Armstrong's gift of the patents was sufficient

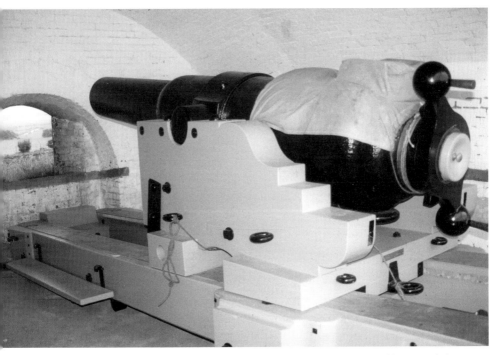

The Armstrong 7in RBL gun, the first British breech-loading gun. This example is mounted at Fort Nelson, the artillery museum at Portsmouth. (*Author's photograph*)

to advance him in the eyes of the British government, and Blakely was reduced to selling his guns overseas.

As it happened, Armstrong's system of breech-loading was not a success, as once again there were problems in successfully sealing the breech on firing. The British authorities decided to carry out a comparative trial of Armstrong's breech-loading and muzzle-loading rifled guns and Whitworth's muzzle-loading rifled gun. Armstrong had modified the action of his breech-loader, and in the trial all the guns performed satisfactorily. However, the committee supervising the trial reported in 1865 that the muzzle-loaders were superior to the breech-loading gun in all respects, including the ease of working the gun and the cost of manufacture.

A series of trials over a period of ten years confirmed the superiority of rifled ordnance over the old smooth-bore guns, but both the Royal Navy and the Army held a vast number of cast iron smooth-bore guns. Attempts had previously been made to convert smooth-bore guns, but without success until Major (later Sir) William Palliser RA proposed a method that was adopted in 1863. This involved lining a cast iron gun that had been bored out for the purpose with an inner tube of coiled iron, mechanically fitted, rifled and expanded into contact with its casing by firing a few rounds. Eventually, three rifled muzzle-loading converted guns were accepted into service. These were the 64pdr 58cwt RML gun converted from the 32pdr SB guns of 58 and 56cwt; the 64pdr 71cwt RML converted from the 8in SB shell gun; and the 80pdr 5 ton RML gun converted from the 68pdr 95cwt SB gun. More than 3,000 smooth-bore guns were subsequently rifled using the Palliser system.

In addition to the work on the converted guns, a new series of muzzle-loading rifled guns was being designed by Armstrong. These were being produced by Armstrong's Elswick Ordnance Factory on the banks of the River Tyne and by the Royal Gun Factory at Woolwich; they used the new 'built-up' system of wrought iron coils on a steel tube. The early guns manufactured by this system and used for coastal defence were the 64pdr 64cwt RML gun; the 7in (177mm) 7 ton RML gun; and the 9in (228mm) 12 ton RML gun. An 8in 12 ton RML gun was also developed but was initially issued for sea service. Subsequently, even larger RML guns were developed, including the 10in 18 ton RML gun used primarily by the Royal Navy; the 11in (279mm) 25 ton RML gun; the 12in 25 ton RML gun; and the 12.5in (317mm) 38 ton RML gun. These last three were used by the army in coastal defence forts, together with two 16in (406mm) RML guns for the famous Dover turret and four huge 17.72in (450mm) 100 ton RML guns, two in Gibraltar and two in Malta.

Although capable of throwing a heavy shell over a distance of up to 5,000yds (4,615m), the effectiveness of these guns was, in fact, measured not by maximum range but by their ability to penetrate armour. Their maximum penetration occurred at relatively short range, with the 7in 7 ton RML gun performing poorly, penetrating 7.9 inches (200mm) of iron at 1,000yds (923m) or 5.9 inches (150mm) at 2,000yds (1,846m). Even the 10in 18 ton gun could only penetrate 11 inches (280mm) of armour at 1,000yds or 9.8 inches (248mm) at 2,000yds.

The 7in 6.5 ton RML gun. Originally approved for sea-service in 1865, being twelve inches shorter than the previous model. A large number were transferred to land-service. The photograph shows one of the guns at Fort Siloso Military Museum in Singapore. (*Author's photograph*)

There were also a number of other drawbacks to the RML guns. They were extremely heavy and cumbersome to operate and had a relatively slow rate of fire. Most were mounted in casemates, and only the smaller 64pdr and 7in guns were suitable for the Moncreiff 'disappearing', or counterweight, mountings, which had recently been introduced. In particular, because of their slow rate of fire, RML guns had to be mounted in large numbers to enable effective fire to be brought on the new steam warships now coming into service. Because of their increased speed and manoeuvrability these ships no longer presented the easy targets which the old sailing line-of-battle ship had.

Advances in the construction of guns were not the only improvements being made to artillery at this time. Gunpowder was now being produced in the form of pellets with a hole in the centre that ensured that the powder burnt more slowly and at a more even rate. This slow-burning powder expended less energy in its initial explosion, so producing a higher muzzle velocity for the shell; but in order to obtain the full effect of this slower combustion a much longer barrel was required. This produced a problem in loading RML guns, particularly those mounted in casemates, since increasing the length of the barrel meant that loading had to take place outside the protection of the casemate.

On the Continent, French and Prussian gun manufacturers, particularly Krupp of Essen, had successfully developed a number of breech-loading guns. At home, Sir William Armstrong was continuing to develop a form of breech-loading using a method known as the 'interrupted screw' to secure the breech and make it gas-tight. Despite these developments, however, the Royal Navy and the Army stuck religiously to muzzle-loading guns, ignoring the evidence of the superiority of breech-loading guns over muzzle-loaders demonstrated first in the Austro-Prussian War of 1866 and then in the Franco-Prussian War of 1870. Eventually, in 1878, the drawbacks of the muzzle-loading system had become so obvious that the Director of Artillery

A 6in Mk VII BL Gun on Central Pivot Mounting Mark II. This gun was to become the mainstay of British coast defence in both the First and Second World Wars. The photograph shows an example at Fort Dunree in Donegal, Ireland. (*Author's photograph*)

submitted a memorandum to the Secretary of State for War saying that, after careful consideration, he had given instructions to the Royal Gun Factory to prepare the design of a breech-loading gun using the interrupted screw breech mechanism.

By the early 1880s breech-loading guns were replacing RML guns in all coastal forts and batteries. The calibres of these guns included 5in (127mm), 6in (152mm), 8in, 9.2in (233mm) and 10in, and the mountings were either *en barbette* or a new hydro-pneumatic system which allowed the gun, mounted in a deep pit, to be loaded in the lowered position and then fired when raised. The guns were fired using a separate bagged charge, and ignition was by means of an electrical current.

These breech-loading guns had a much improved penetration of armour when compared to the older rifled muzzle-loaders. The 6in BL gun could penetrate 8.75 inches (222mm) of armour at 1,000yds (923m) or 5 inches (127mm) at 4,000yds (3,692m), while the performance of the 8in BL gun was even better, penetrating 12.5 inches (317mm) of armour at 1,000yds (923m), or 7.5 inches (190mm) at 4,000yds (3,693m).

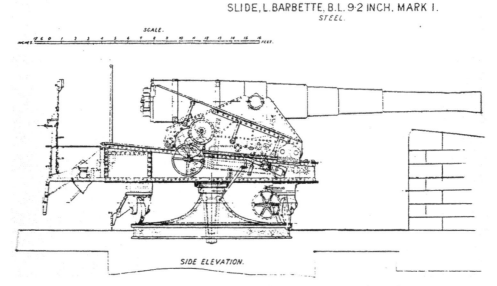

SLIDE, L.BARBETTE. B.L. 9·2 INCH. MARK I.
STEEL.

SCALE.

SIDE ELEVATION.

A drawing of the 9.2in Mk IV BL gun on a Mark II barbette mounting. These guns were replaced by the more modern Mark X just before the First World War. (*Author's collection*)

As well as the heavy breech-loading guns for coastal defence, a lighter weapon, termed a 'quick-firer', was developed to provide a more rapid rate of fire, particularly to counteract attacks on shipping by the new fast torpedo boats. The first quick-firing guns to be developed fired fixed ammunition, that is a warhead, either a 3lb (1.36kg) or a 6lb (2.72kg) shell, attached to a brass cartridge case containing the propellant and the ignition primer. The rate of fire of these guns was much faster than that of the heavier breech-loaders: with trained gun crews, the 3pdr could fire thirty and the 6pdr twenty-five rounds per minute. However, as the size of torpedo boats increased, a gun firing a heavier shell was required in order to inflict significant damage on them, and so the 12pdr QF gun was developed, followed, finally, by the 4.7in (119mm) and the 6in (152mm). Both were originally naval weapons, but the 4.7in gun, introduced in 1888 and firing a shell weighing 45lbs (20kg), was widely adopted for coastal defence use.

So, in twenty-five years there had been great advances in the construction and effectiveness of guns, brought about to a large extent by the need to counteract the revolutionary changes that had taken place in the construction of warships occurring in the same period.

The Forts and Batteries

The superiority of rifled guns over smooth-bore ordnance had been proved in a number of trials. The new guns had a higher muzzle velocity, were more accurate and could deliver an extremely destructive projectile. What had not been tested was the effectiveness of these weapons against masonry fortifications. Defence against smooth-bore artillery had been achieved by building thicker walls of stone or brick. Many coastal fortifications were of considerable height, allowing two and sometimes three tiers of guns, which enabled their slow rate of fire to be compensated for by the number available to fire at a target.

A number of forces, including the British Army, wished to discover exactly how effective the new rifled guns were when used against masonry. In 1860 the War Department used Martello towers Nos 49 and 71 on the Sussex coast for a comparative study of the effects of the old and the new guns when fired against a masonry structure. In the same year, the Prussian army

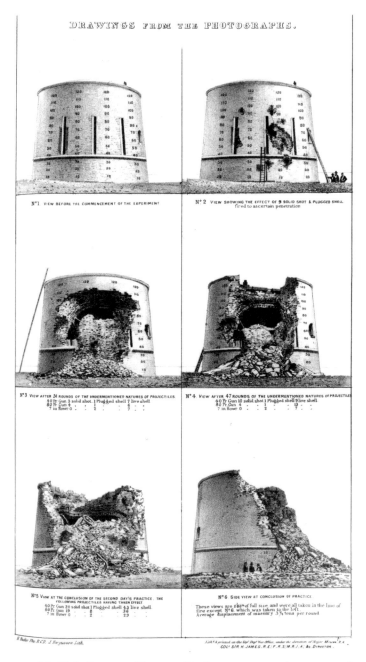

Martello tower No 71 in Pevensey Bay near Eastbourne was used as a target in artillery trials in 1860. The drawing, taken from contemporary photographs, shows the progressive damage from the fire of rifled guns. (*Author's collection*)

carried out a similar trial against the walls of the small fortress of Juliers; and at this time the French were also experimenting and carried out their trials at Vincennes.

For the British tests, 32pdr and 68pdr smooth-bore guns were used against Martello tower No 49, while three of the new rifled guns, an Armstrong 7in RBL firing a shell weighing 100lb (45kg), a rifled 40pdr muzzle-loader and a rifled 80pdr muzzle-loader were used against Martello tower No 71 near Eastbourne. The tests were conclusive: No 71 was quickly demolished, while No 49 was damaged but still serviceable.

The introduction of rifled guns and steamships by the French had alarmed the British public, and as a result of newspaper pressure the British government was forced, in 1859, to set up a Royal Commission to consider the matter of defence of the naval ports. The Royal Commission reported in early 1860 and, as a result of its recommendations, a huge programme of defence works was put in hand to defend the United Kingdom's major naval bases. The new forts proposed by the Royal Commission were to have brick or stone gorge walls, while the front and flank defences were earthwork ramparts 50ft (15.4m) thick and faced with brick or stone. Below the ramparts there were casemates, arched chambers with one or two gun embrasures and a bomb-proof roof. On top of the rampart additional guns were to be mounted, firing through embrasures or from Haxo casemates, the latter being brick gun shelters covered with earth, open at the rear and with an embrasure at the front which were named after their inventor, the French military engineer, General Haxo.

The American Civil War proved quite conclusively that the old Vauban-style masonry fortifications could not withstand the bombardment of rifled guns. Instead, the armies on both sides of the conflict developed earthwork defences that proved more effective in absorbing much of the impact of the new rifled projectiles. As a result, British military engineers moved towards a greater use of earth embankments, usually laid out in an irregular pentagon according to the ground on which the fort was situated.

The use of a casemate to protect the gun and its crew had the disadvantage that it limited the traverse of the gun. Mounting a gun in an open position firing *en barbette* was more effective, since it permitted the gun to traverse over a greater arc, and these positions were cheaper to construct. However,

Aerial photograph of Crownhill Fort in Plymouth, one of the new style of forts built as a result of the Royal Commission of 1860 to withstand the fire of rifled artillery. (*Courtesy of the Landmark Trust*)

the British military authorities of the 1860s believed that such positions were vulnerable to fire from an enemy ship and that the gun crew was particularly vulnerable when reloading a muzzle-loader. An answer to this problem was suggested by Captain Moncreiff, an officer of the Edinburgh Militia Artillery, who designed a counterweight mounting which enabled a gun to be loaded by its crew within a gun pit. The gun was raised to its firing position by releasing the counterweight; then, when the gun fired, the recoil forced the weight upwards causing the gun to sink back into the pit for reloading. Although the Moncreiff mounting ensured protection for the gun crew, it had the disadvantage of slowing the rate of fire. Nevertheless, the mounting was adopted by the War Department for use in a number of land forts; it was mainly used with the 64pdr RML and the 7in RBL guns, but did not prove successful with the larger RML guns.

By the mid-1880s Sir William Armstrong's new breech-loading guns were being introduced into service, and with their improved rate of fire when compared to the old RML guns there was a move to mount these guns in open pits firing *en barbette*. Senior officers failed to appreciate the fact that it would always be difficult for a gun on an unstable platform (a ship) to hit a smaller target (the gun pit), nor did they really appreciate the fact that the crews of breech-loading guns were less exposed as they were working in the gun pit. Consequently, they now looked for a new form of mounting.

To meet the War Department's new requirement, the Elswick Ordnance Company, Sir William Armstrong's firm, produced a 'disappearing' mounting for the 6in, the 8in and the 10in BL guns, using a hydro-pneumatic system rather than a simple counterweight. An armoured shield covered the top of the gun pit, with an aperture to permit the gun to be raised through the shield to its firing position, while the shield provided added protection for the gun crew from shrapnel.

The new breech-loading guns brought about a further change in the development of coastal defence forts. These now consisted of concrete gun positions for two or more guns, with underground magazines between the gun positions. Each battery had one or two positions for Depression Range Finder (DRF) equipment, and the gun positions were usually protected from attack on the landward side by walls, ditches, and 'unclimbable' metal fences. The ditches were defended by *caponiers* and counterscarp galleries. The building material was now reinforced concrete rather than brick or masonry, and soon the landward defences were supplemented with barbed wire entanglement fences.

All these developments were to have their effect on the defences of Singapore as the nineteenth century gradually grew to a close and Singapore grew in importance as a port and naval base.

Chapter 4

The First Rifled Guns: 1870–1880

In 1868 Sir Edward Cardwell was appointed Secretary of State for War, a position he held until 1874. Cardwell was a reformer, abolishing the system by which Army officers' commissions were purchased, reducing the term of enlistment for private soldiers to six years and making the office of Secretary of State for War superior to the Commander-in-Chief of the army, at that time the Duke of Cambridge, the Queen's first cousin. In addition, he withdrew Imperial troops from the self-governing colonies in a move to reduce the cost of these garrisons to the Army's annual Estimates.

But while the War Office looked for ways in which the cost of the Estimates could be reduced, technological change in the construction of artillery was making the armament and fortifications of Singapore obsolete; at the same time, the chances of the colony being subject to external aggression

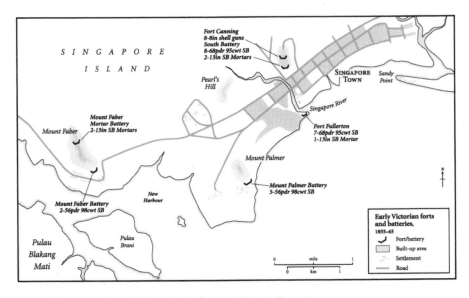

Map of Singapore's early Victorian defences. (*Martin Brown*)

increased, with the rise of the newly unified Germany and an expansionist Russia.

Having previously been Secretary of State for the Colonies, Cardwell was well placed to assess the defence requirements of Singapore. In 1869 he consulted Colonel William Drummond Jervois RE, then Deputy Director of Works and Fortifications at the War Office. Jervois could see no external threat to Singapore and believed that the colony should only be defended against casual naval attack. He therefore recommended that both Fort Fullerton and the battery on Mount Palmer be abandoned, and that proceeds from the sale of the land on which Fort Fullerton stood should be used to fund new works on Mount Faber and a floating battery in the harbour. One can only assume that Jervois believed the sale of the Fort Fullerton site, in the middle of the commercial district of the town, would generate a substantial sum of money. With the reduction of the fixed defences of the colony, reliance would now have to be placed entirely on a Royal Navy armed steamer and a number of small gunboats, supported by 'torpedoes', an archaic term for electrically detonated mines.

Jervois' proposals were strongly opposed by the Governor of the day, Major General Sir Harry St George Ord. Governor Ord did not believe that the Royal Navy would be happy to dedicate a warship simply to the defence of Singapore, and was consequently of the opinion that coastal batteries would still be required. Ord did not get his way, but his opposition did re-open the question of the size of the colony's garrison, and in 1871 this was finally settled at one European regiment and one battery of artillery; the colonial contribution was set at £51,595, with the colony itself undertaking additional military expenditure of approximately £7,000 per annum. It was also agreed that one wing of a European regiment, the 10th Foot, should be stationed in the colony but should be available for general service elsewhere in the Far East.

Four years after the reduction in the size of the garrison, the commanding officer in China, Major General Whitfield, forwarded a confidential report to the War Office in which he stated that the forts and batteries in Singapore were quite incapable of withstanding the fire of modern artillery. To provide an effective defence of the town and harbour the existing works needed to be rebuilt and new ones constructed. All this should only be undertaken after a comprehensive review of the whole policy of defence for Singapore.

The debate over the size of the garrison might have continued for a number of years had it not been for developments in Central Asia. In the twelve years from 1864 to 1876 Russia thrust aggressively into the region, annexing Turkestan, Tashkent, Samarkand, Khiva, Bukhara and Kokand. The steady advance of Russian forces across Central Asia was seen in London as a developing threat to British India, and in 1874 the new Tory government of Benjamin Disraeli was deeply distrustful of Russia. Disraeli was determined to strengthen British foreign and imperial policy, particularly in regard to Russia, and relations between the two countries rapidly cooled.

In 1875 Sir William Drummond Jervois, now late of the War Office Department of Works and Fortifications, was appointed Governor of the Straits Settlements colony. Perhaps not surprisingly, with his appointment as Governor Jervois changed his view of the colony's defence requirements. In August 1876 he presented a report to the Colonial Office that recommended a radically different approach from his earlier view.

In this report Jervois emphasized the present commercial importance of Singapore and, in particular, its vital role as a coaling station for both warships of the Royal Navy and merchant vessels:

> [It is] of the utmost importance that Singapore should be secured against such attack as might be made upon it by a hostile cruizer [sic] or a small squadron of vessels. The harbour would thus be made a secure base of operations for the fleet, and the centre of commercial operations of Great Britain in the Eastern Archipelago would be protected.[1]

Jervois dismissed the existing fortifications as weak and insignificant, and he was particularly damning in his description of Fort Canning, which he said was a 'straggling work', the trace of which followed the top contour of the hill. He continued:

> It is unprovided with flank defence; the parapets are weak and badly proportioned; the ditch is shallow and insignificant; the scarp and counterscarp are only partially swept by musketry fire from the parapet;

the magazines are not bombproof and are much exposed; and there is, moreover, little or no bombproof cover for the garrison ... the guns with which it is armed require re-venting and the wooden carriages and platforms, upon which they are mounted, have all suffered from exposure to climate.[2]

Jervois therefore considered that Fort Canning should be retained simply as a defence work for the protection of the town in conjunction with the redoubt on Mount Faber and an intermediate field redoubt, with a redistribution of the armament so that it commanded the town. Nor did Jervois consider Fort Fullerton or the battery on Mount Palmer to have any merit as defensive fortifications; it would seem that the battery on Mount Faber was in a ruinous condition at that time.

Jervois' plan was to construct a number of new forts and batteries that would mount the new large muzzle-loading, rifled guns currently coming into service in the British Army. For the defence of the New Harbour he proposed two new fortifications on Blakang Mati, one on Mount Serapong

A view of Fort Canning c. 1885. The photograph shows the Officers' Quarters and the flagstaff, with South Battery at a lower level in front. (*TNA CO 1069/484*)

This photograph, dated 1882, shows one of the Fort Palmer gun positions together with a 7in 6.5 ton RML gun. Two traverses, each containing a magazine, are also in the picture. (*TNA CO 1069/484*)

at the eastern end and the other on Mount Siloso at the western end of the island. In addition, there was to be a new battery on Mount Palmer to replace the existing work, and the battery on Mount Faber was to be rebuilt.

The Mount Serapong fort was to be the largest of the proposed new works and was to be built round a knoll that crowned the summit of the hill and would act as a traverse protecting the armament of ten 11in 25 ton RML guns from fire from the rear. The other fortification on the island, the battery on Mount Siloso, was to be an open battery armed with six 11in 25 ton RML guns and sited to bring fire to bear on any enemy vessel attempting to enter the New Harbour from the west.

A new Fort Palmer was to be placed on the summit of the hill at a height of about 110ft (33m) above sea level, and it was to be armed with four 11in RML guns. Jervois also recommended that the gorge of the fort be designed to mount two or three small calibre guns to provide flanking fire on to the northern slopes of Mount Faber and to enfilade the valley stretching in front of it. In this manner, the fort would be able to co-operate with the Mount Serapong fort in defending the eastern entrance to the New Harbour.

To further protect the town from any attack from the rear by an enemy landing force Jervois also proposed that two redoubts be built on Mount Faber, one to be placed on the north-western extremity of the range at a height of 350ft (107m) and the other on the south-eastern spur above the site of the existing Mount Faber battery.

Finally, Jervois proposed that a battery armed with five 11in RML guns should be constructed near Tanjong Katong, east of the town, to prevent enemy ships approaching the New Harbour from that direction. In addition, he recommended that electrically-operated mines ('torpedoes') should be used to close the approaches to the New Harbour.

The design Jervois suggested for the new fortifications was to be that of the Upper Battery on Drake's Island in Plymouth Harbour. This Upper, or Main, Battery had five *en barbette* emplacements for two 12in and three 11in 25 ton RML guns, each separated by a vaulted, earth-covered magazine with, underneath, a series of alternating cartridge and shell stores. Access was to be by means of a passage to the rear, and at the rear there was also to be a main underground magazine.

The overall cost of Colonel Jervois' plan for the fortifications of the colony came to £130,000 or, as he said at the conclusion to his report, 'less than the cost of one ironclad turret vessel'.[3]

Jervois left Singapore in 1877 on his appointment as defence adviser to the Australian colonies (he subsequently became Governor of South Australia). His report on the defences, however, did not languish pigeon-holed in London as had so many earlier reports. The European political scene in 1877 was in a ferment after Russia had gone to war with Turkey over the Ottoman government's attempts to suppress nationalist uprisings in the Balkans and its persecution of its Christian subjects. The war was brought to an end in 1878 with the Treaty of San Stefano, which gave Russia unrestricted right of passage for its Black Sea Fleet into the Mediterranean. The British government, however, refused to recognize the treaty and warned Russia that there would be war between the two countries if the offending clause was not withdrawn.

In March 1878 the government in London established the Colonial Defence Committee as part of its preparation for war, and the Colonial Office instructed the Governors of the respective colonies each to set up a Local Defence Committee comprising the principal military officers in the colony and to review their defences in view of the threatening aspect of European affairs. Governor Robinson in Singapore instructed the senior military officers in the colony to report on its defences, estimating the likely threat as being from a small enemy squadron of warships or a single unarmoured cruiser.

In the following month the Local Defence Committee submitted a scathing report, in which it declared that the existing armament of the colony would be useless against an enemy warship and that, anyway, most of the guns were unserviceable. In the words of the Local Defence Committee report: 'Any defence of the New Harbour approaches with any of the present armament or with torpedoes would be both futile and injudicious without the roadstead being also defended.'[4] In the immediate term, the Local Defence Committee planned to repair and remount seven 68pdr SB guns of the existing armament, siting three guns in the existing Fort Palmer, two guns in the lower battery on Mount Faber, and two guns in a sandbag battery to be built at Tanjong Katong.

Only a few days after receiving the Local Defence Committee's report, the Colonial Defence Committee in London reviewed the position and produced its 'Report on the Temporary Defences of Singapore'. In view of the importance of Singapore to British trade, the value of which passing through Singapore having been estimated at £78 million per annum, and the value of the coal stocks there, currently noted as being unguarded, the committee decided that immediate steps should be taken to strengthen the colony's defences.

These immediate steps took the form of authorization for the dispatch of ten 7in (177mm) 7 ton RML guns and six 64pdr RML guns. Eight of the 7in guns were destined for the two new batteries to be built on Blakang Mati, five on Mount Siloso and three on Mount Serapong. The remaining two 7in guns were to be placed in the existing battery on Mount Palmer prior to the construction of a new battery on the hill. The 64pdr guns were 'to be distributed among those works at the discretion of the military authorities on the post'.[5]

The Colonial Defence Committee also authorized the construction of an additional self-defensible battery at Tanjong Katong. This battery was to mount three 7in 7 ton RML guns and was designed to assist in the protection of the roadstead and the town. In addition, a battery for two 64pdr RML guns was authorized for Teregeh Point on Pulau Brani. Further protection was to be provided by the installation of 'torpedoes', and the Royal Navy was asked to provide a warship and two gunboats of the *Comet* class. These latter were small 'flatiron' boats of 250 tons displacement, with a speed of 10 knots and armed with a single 10in (254mm) 18 ton RML gun. The total cost of the new armament, works of fortification and two gunboats came to a total of £62,200, less than half that of Jervois' scheme.

The War Office notified the Colonial Office that six of the heavy guns and half the ammunition for them had left London in June 1878 by sailing vessel; the remaining guns would follow by steamer. The War Office agreed that the seven serviceable 68pdr SB guns from the existing batteries should be distributed to the new batteries as proposed by the Colonial Defence

Officers and men involved in building the Singapore defences in 1878. (*The Wellcome Foundation*)

Committee. Those guns removed from Fort Canning were to be replaced by such serviceable 8in (203mm) SB guns 'as may be available to meet any local disturbance'.[6] However, the local commander Royal Artillery, Lieutenant Colonel Hall RA, disagreed with this proposal, maintaining that the guns on Mount Palmer would be unable to cover the north–eastern entrance to the New Harbour and would be unsupported by the fire of other guns. He also pointed out that the lower battery on Mount Faber was in a dilapidated condition and only one gun would be able to bear on the entrance to the New Harbour, so the value of the second gun would be very slight.

To add to the problem, it appeared that the existing embrasures restricted the guns' lateral range. Colonel Hall also believed the performance of the 64pdr 58cwt Palliser-converted RML gun to be inferior to that of the wrought iron 64pdr, since the former was not able to fire the 90lb (40kg) battering shell. However, the 7in RML gun was a considerably more powerful piece than the older 68pdr 95cwt SB gun which it was replacing in Singapore. The maximum range of the 7in gun was 5,000yds (4,615m), compared to a range

This photograph, dating from the 1880s, shows two of the 68pdr 95cwt SB guns of South Battery with an associated magazine. (*TNA CO 1069/484*)

of 3,000yds (2,770m) for the 68pdr SB. More importantly, however, the 7in RML was capable of penetrating 7in (17.5cm) of armour at 1,000yds (923m).

In the light of the dispatch of the new rifled guns from England and their imminent arrival in Singapore, the Local Defence Committee decided that only three of the old 68pdr SB guns planned to be remounted would be mounted; these would be in the Fort Palmer battery, and the two 56pdr SB guns already there would be left in place.

In August 1878 work was in progress to construct the new batteries on Mount Serapong and Mount Siloso on Blakang Mati, and in January 1879 the land for the Tanjong Katong self-defensible battery and the new Mount Palmer battery was purchased and the design for the Mount Palmer battery agreed.[7]

In London, Lord Carnarvon, the Secretary of State for the Colonies in the Disraeli government, ordered a review of the defence arrangements for each colony. The Carnarvon Commission, or the 'Royal Commission Appointed to Enquire into the Defence of British Possessions and Commerce Abroad', to give it its formal title, was set up in 1879. A Royal Engineers officer, Colonel William Crossman, who was known to Lord Carnarvon from the earlier Royal Commission into the Black Flag Rebellion in Griqualand West, South Africa, was dispatched on behalf of the Commission to report on the defences of the principal colonies.

Crossman had been the assistant director of Fortifications and Works in the War Office and then the officer in charge of submarine mining, so he was well qualified to report on colonial defences. His report considered the position in Singapore under two headings:

a. Defence of the New Harbour (docks and coaling wharves).
b. Protection of the roadstead and the town north of the Singapore River.

At the time of his report, work had been completed on a number of the new batteries authorized by the Colonial Defence Committee in 1878. Those included the new battery on Mount Siloso on Blakang Mati which was to be armed with three 7in 6.5 ton RML guns and two 64pdr 58cwt Palliser-converted RML guns. It would seem that 7in 6.5 ton guns had been substituted for the 7 ton guns originally proposed because at that time the 6.5 ton guns were the only spare pieces available for the defence of the colonies, a large number of sea-service guns having been made available for land service by the Royal Navy.

The Mount Siloso battery was to defend the western approach to the New Harbour and was constructed by levelling part of the summit of the hill. The works were supervised by Lieutenant Henry McCallum RE, who was seconded from his post as Superintendent of Admiralty Harbour Works at Hong Kong in order to oversee the project. Lieutenant (soon to be Captain) McCallum was concerned that a small knoll interfered with the ability of one of the 7in RML guns and the two 64pdr RML guns to sweep the area of the minefield with fire. His very economical solution was to remove the knoll and prepare a *glacis* by using 19,000lb of condemned gunpowder in a number of mine galleries This he did successfully, and subsequently reported on the feat in an article in the *Journal of the Royal Engineers*.[8]

The second battery on Blakang Mati, known as Blakang Mati East, was to be armed with four 7in RML guns and two 64pdr RML guns; this, together with the new Mount Palmer battery, protected the eastern approach to the New Harbour. The armament of the Mount Palmer battery was to be the same as that on Mount Siloso.

The battery on Mount Siloso was under construction when Crossman visited Singapore. Indeed, there had been a further alteration to its proposed armament in the interim: it was now to consist of two 7in RML guns and 'two pieces of heavier calibre', together with a single 64pdr RML.[9] A subsequent War Office memorandum dated 20 November 1880 proposed a further change to the battery's armament so that it was now to comprise three 10in (254mm) 18 ton RML guns and two 64pdr RMLs.

Colonel Crossman, like most Royal Engineers officers tasked with designing coastal defences, could not resist the opportunity to produce a most elaborate scheme without giving much or, indeed, any consideration to eventual cost. He reviewed the existing defences and recommended three new batteries and a sea fort, together with further improvements to the existing works. He also supported the recommendation in the War Office memorandum that the existing batteries should be re-armed with 10in 18 ton RML guns.

For the existing batteries on Blakang Mati Crossman proposed the removal of additional rock at Point Rimeau adjoining the Mount Siloso battery to enable two additional 10in RML guns to be mounted, thus increasing the armament recommended in the War Office memorandum from three 10in guns to five such pieces and two of the smaller 64pdr RML guns. Two guns, one 10in and one 64pdr RML, were to be sited on the left flank of the reconstructed battery to enable fire to be brought to bear on the southern shore of Blakang Mati, while the second 64pdr gun was to be positioned to flank a proposed submarine minefield. The remaining guns of the battery would bring converging fire on the approaches to the western entrance to New Harbour.

The other existing battery on Blakang Mati was the East Battery on the south-eastern slopes of Mount Serapong, at that time armed with two 7in 7 ton and one 64pdr RML guns. The War Office memorandum had recommended the re-arming of this battery with five 10in 18 ton RML guns and one 64pdr, and Crossman supported this change in armament. However, the Local Defence Committee believed that the waters south of Blakang Mati were insufficiently covered by fire and recommended lengthening the right flank of the existing East Battery in order to provide space for additional guns. The Government Engineer, Captain McCallum RE, when asked to advise, advocated the construction of an entirely new battery on the southern shore of the island some 900yds (830m) from Mount Serapong, and Colonel Crossman endorsed this view.

In addition to these suggested improvements to the existing batteries, Crossman believed it would be necessary to construct a number of new batteries to ensure the defence of both the eastern and western entrances to New Harbour. In order to increase the number of guns defending the western entrance he proposed a battery to be sited at Pasir Panjang near Berlayer Point, opposite Mount Siloso. The battery was to mount three 10in 18 ton RML guns and two 64pdr RML guns, with a third 64pdr sited to bear on the submarine minefield. This gun would complement the similar piece also covering the minefield from Blakang Mati. This battery was to be made secure against assault.

The battery on Mount Palmer was dismissed by Colonel Crossman as being 'too far retired from the channel that it does not afford the close defence which is desirable'.[10] So his suggestion was that a new battery for three 10in 18 ton RML guns and one 64pdr should be built on the dock wall at Tanjong Paggar to replace the Mount Palmer Battery. However, if his proposal to build the dock wall battery was not approved, then the Mount Palmer Battery should be modified to enable it to mount a heavier armament comprising four 10in 18 ton RML guns and two 64pdrs. The heavy guns were to be sited so as to bring fire to bear on the entrance to the harbour, and the lighter guns were to fire towards Fort Canning.

For defence of the eastern entrance Crossman recommended removing the 7in 6.5 ton RML guns from the battery at Tanjong Katong and replacing them with three 10in 18 ton RML guns; also constructing a sea fort, similar to those in the Solent off Portsmouth, to mount five 10in RML guns. This latter proposal was a particularly ambitious one which, as we will see, would add considerably to the cost of Crossman's proposed defences.

Finally, in order to protect the landward approach to the batteries on Blakang Mati and the town of Singapore itself, Crossman proposed the construction of a number of infantry redoubts and the retention of Fort Canning as a defensive work. On Blakang Mati a small infantry redoubt was proposed on Mount Imbeah, capable of being held by half a company of infantry with a machine gun, while the existing redoubt on Mount Serapong was to be enlarged and armed with three 40pdr RML 'guns of position'.

To defend the landward approach to the town Crossman agreed with the War Office memorandum that the work on Mount Faber should be retained as an enclosed position for a garrison of 200 men and four 64pdr RML guns. He also recommended that Fort Canning should continue to be garrisoned and armed with four 64pdr guns and that the old smooth-bore armament currently in the fort should be retained. To defend the area between Mount Faber and Fort Canning he proposed a number of small intermediate field redoubts, each for a garrison of fifty men and two 40pdr RML 'guns of position'.

The garrison of Singapore at this time consisted of two companies of the Royal Artillery, a battalion of native infantry and a wing of a British infantry regiment. The number of gunners in this force would, quite clearly, be inadequate to man the new batteries and redoubts proposed by Crossman. His solution was that three companies of Indian gunners with British officers should be raised, similar to the company of gun lascars recruited for the defences of Hong Kong.

Colonel Crossman completed his review of the Singapore defences with the recommendation that two submarine minefields should be installed to protect New Harbour, using sixteen 500lb (227kg) ground mines and thirty eight electro-contact mines, with a firing station at Tanjong Pagar.

In summary Crossman's plan for the defence comprised:

Passir Panjang (Berlayer Point)	3 x 10in 18 ton RML
	3 x 64pdr RML
Mount Siloso	5 x 10in 18 ton RML
	2 x 64pdr RML
Blakang Mati East	5 x 10in18 ton RML
	1 x 64pdr RML
Blakang Mati South	3 x 7in 6.5 ton RML
Tanjong Katong	3 x 10in 18 ton RML
Mount Palmer	4 x 10in18 ton RML
	2 x 64pdr RML
Tanjong Paggar (Dock Wall)	3 x 10in 18 ton RML
Sea Fort	6 x 10in 18 ton RML
Fort Canning	4 x 64pdr RML
Mount Faber Redoubt	4 x 64pdr RML
Mount Serapong Redoubt	3 x 40pdr 35cwt RML
Intermediate Field Redoubts	2 x 40pdr 35 cwt RML each

Crossman estimated the total cost of the proposed fortifications for the New Harbour to be approximately £148,000 if the Dock Wall Battery at Tanjong Paggar was to be built. The reconstruction of the battery at Tanjong Katong and the ambitious plan for a sea fort would add a further £144,000, making a grand total of £292,000. This was a quite extraordinarily large sum for the defence of a small, albeit important, colony.[11]

Needless to say, both the War Office and the Colonial Office baulked at these figures; indeed, the War Office made every effort to offload the costs of maintaining the Singapore defences on to the Colonial Office. Negotiations continued until 1885, when an agreement was reached under which the Colonial Office accepted financial responsibility for the fortifications, while the War Office undertook to build and maintain the submarine minefields.

The only known photograph of the original Fort Tanjong Katong, showing the rear of the battery and two traverses containing expense magazines for the 7in 6.5 ton RML guns. (*The Wellcome Foundation*)

Chapter 5

Bureaucrats and Breech-loaders: 1881–1900

The annexation of Kokand in 1876 did not slake the Russians' thirst for expansion in Central Asia. Their next move came in 1881, when they besieged and captured the fortress town of Geok Tepe, today in Turkmenistan; three years later they moved again to capture the large oasis and town of Merv, some 200 miles (320km) west of Geok Tepe. The British government saw this advance towards the Afghanistan border as a threat to India, and any further advance southwards from Merv would undoubtedly ring alarm bells in London and Calcutta. In 1885 Russian forces defeated an Afghan army detachment in the Battle of Kishka and seized the oasis of Panjdeh, south of the River Oxus and on the road to the major Afghan city of Herat, so initiating a major Anglo-Russian crisis.

What became known as the 'Panjdeh Incident' was subsequently defused diplomatically, assisted by the fact that the Emir of Afghanistan, prompted by Lord Dufferin, the Viceroy of India, whom he was visiting at the time, accepted this action as no more than a trivial border incident. No doubt the Emir was also fully aware that any war between Britain and Russia would be waged across his territory to the detriment of himself and his people. As a result of these negotiations Russia was permitted to retain Merv and Panjdeh, while the Emir retained Zulfihar, a pass through a gorge of the Hari Rud River, together with Gulran and Meruchak.

Meanwhile, concern at the inadequate defences of Singapore was exacerbated when Sir Andrew Clarke, the Inspector General of Fortifications in London and a former Governor of the colony, rather surprisingly proposed limiting the fortifications of Singapore simply to those required for the defence of New Harbour. Needless to say, this was not acceptable to the rapidly growing British population of the colony, who felt that if war should come Singapore would be vulnerable to attack by the Russian Pacific fleet.

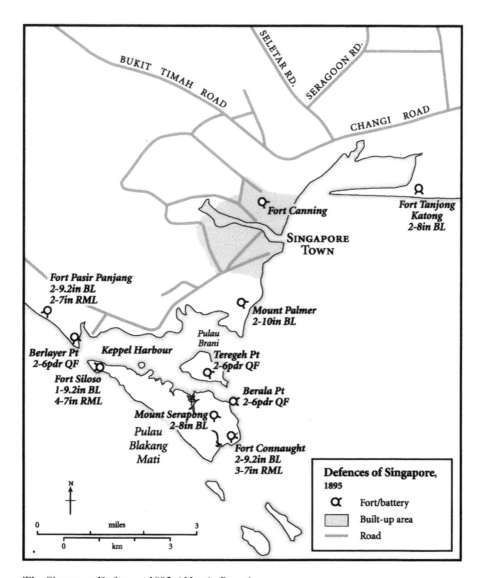

The Singapore Defences, 1895. (*Martin Brown*)

The local press in Singapore was voluble in its support of improved defences for the town and harbour, described in a report of 1882 as comprising the earthwork batteries at Mount Siloso, the open earthwork battery at Blakang Mati East and the two masonry and earthwork forts, Fort Palmer and Fort Tanjong Katong, the latter also protected by a wet ditch. The acting

Governor, Cecil Smith, proposed to London that Fort Tanjong Katong be re-armed as a matter of urgency, since the Local Defence Committee had described the existing armament of the fort as outdated and virtually useless against modern warships. The acting Governor's recommendation was that the fort should be equipped with one 10in (254mm) BL gun and two 9in (233mm) RML guns.[1] The Governor, Sir Frederick Weld, who was in England at this time, also urged the Colonial Office to dispatch extra guns immediately.

As we have seen in the previous chapter, the Carnarvon Commission's recommendation in 1882 was that the colony should be armed with a total of ten 10in RML guns, three 7in (177mm) RML guns, seven 64pdr RML guns and a number of 40pdr RML 'guns of position'. The Inspector General of Fortifications disagreed with this proposal and proposed instead that the 10in RML guns should be replaced by the latest 9.2in (233mm) BL guns and that the number of RML guns should be reduced.

The War Office, acting on the request of the Colonial Office, reviewed the existing defences of the colony and authorized an improvement which involved the construction of a new battery on Mount Serapong on Blakang Mati, on the site of the existing infantry redoubt. Improvements were also authorized to the existing works in order to permit the mounting of additional and more modern ordnance.

The guns authorized by the War Office to be sent to Singapore comprised:

2 x 10in Mk III BL guns on *barbette* mountings Mk I
9 x 9.2in Mk IV BL guns on *barbette* mountings Mk I
8 x 7in RML guns
7 x 64pdr RML guns

The problem, however, was that both the 10in and 9.2in BL guns were still under development at this time; indeed, the 10in gun was not to be approved for service until October 1888.

Although the Panjdeh Incident had duly subsided, the inadequacy of the colony's defences continued to concern its inhabitants. Their belief that Singapore was virtually undefended was further underlined in 1885 by the arrival in Singapore of four Russian warships in transit to join the

Russian Pacific Fleet. The vessels were the armoured cruisers *General Admiral, Vladimir-Monomac,* and *Minin,* each armed with 8in (203mm) BL guns, and the sloop *Opritsnik,* armed with 6in (152mm) BL guns. It was clear to the inhabitants of Singapore that the guns mounted on these vessels were all superior in performance to the ordnance currently defending Singapore.

Since none of the new heavy breech-loading guns were available at this time from either the Royal Gun Factory at Woolwich or from Armstrong's Elswick factory in Newcastle, as they were still under development, the War Office was forced to shop around for what was available worldwide. The result was that in May 1885, four months after the Russian ships had passed through Singapore, approval was given for the purchase of four Armstrong 8in BL guns from the Viceroy of Canton; these were shipped, complete with mountings, to Hong Kong.[2] The Canton Provincial Government had purchased one of these guns from Armstrong's in 1879 for £1,760, but there is no record of what the British government paid for them.[3]

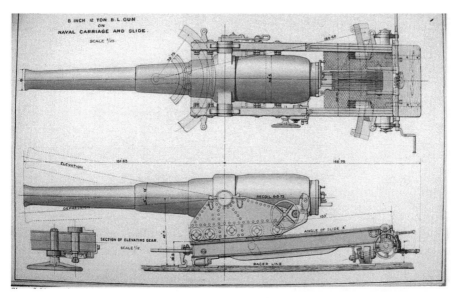

Drawing of an Armstrong 8in BL gun, two of which were mounted in Fort Tanjong Katong and two in Fort Serapong. The engraving shows the gun on a naval broadside mounting rather than the barbette carriage used for the guns in the two Singapore forts. (*Author's collection*)

Two of these four guns were to be mounted in Fort Tanjong Katong and two in the new fort being built on Mount Serapong. Despite plans for the necessary modifications to Fort Tanjong Katong being sent out in July 1885, delays in the construction of the fort on Mount Serapong and the modification of Fort Tanjong Katong, together with inter-service rivalry, meant that the guns were not actually installed until 1890. In 1891 one of the guns burst on firing, and instructions were issued that the 8in BL guns should only be fired in an emergency.[4]

As a result of the purchase from China, the War Office reduced the number of 9.2in guns to be delivered to Singapore from nine to seven. The allocation of the additional guns to the fortifications was to be as follows:

a.	Fort Palmer	2 x 10in Mk III BL guns on *barbette* mountings Mk I
b.	Fort Siloso	1 x 9.2in Mk IV BL gun on *barbette* mounting Mk I
		4 x 7in 6.5 ton RML guns
c.	Fort Pasir Panjang	2 x 9.2in Mk IV BL guns on *barbette* mountings Mk I
		2 x 7in 6.5 ton RML guns
d.	Blakang Mati East	2 x 9.2in Mk IV BL guns on *barbette* Battery mountings Mk I
		3 x 7in 6.5 ton RML guns
e.	Teregeh Point	2 x 64pdr 64cwt RML guns

Teregeh Point was a new battery, whose role was to cover the eastern minefield that defended New Harbour. In addition, four 64pdr RML guns were to be mounted in the South Battery at Fort Canning. The breech-loading guns were to be mounted *en barbette* instead of on hydro-pneumatic mountings which were used for similar calibre guns in Australia, New Zealand and South Africa. The total cost of the new armaments, including the four 8in BL guns came to £42,000, with an additional £75,000 for the defence works in which they were to be mounted.

The new defence works were to be supervised by the Colonial Engineer, Major Henry McCallum RE, as there was no Military Works Department in

Singapore at that time and the War Office was unable to provide Royal Engineer staff to establish one, though plans would be dispatched from London. Work on the forts to enable them to mount the new armament meant that work on Fort Palmer was delayed while the other forts were modified, since only Fort Palmer was able to defend the eastern entrance to New Harbour while construction of the new works took place.

Delays in the production and dispatch of the new breech-loading guns gave rise to further frustration in Singapore. As late as 1894 the GOC was writing to the Governor, Sir Charles Maxwell, to complain that, 'The defences cannot be considered satisfactory until BL guns are substituted for the 7in RML and QF guns for the 64pdr guns. The 7in

Major Henry McCallum, the Colonial Engineer in Singapore 1884–97. (*Author's collection*)

RML gun is generally uncertain and often erratic in its performances.' This problem arose, apparently, from difficulty in traversing the 7in guns when the racer became wet or greasy after heavy rain, since the traversing lever had a tendency to slip and would not bite on the rail when pressure was applied. In reply the Governor stated, 'With such slow training and laying it would be much better to throw the guns into the sea, as their being reckoned in the defence was misleading.'[5]

While work was in progress to re-arm the defences of Singapore an increasingly acrimonious argument developed between the Straits Settlements and the Colonial Office in London over the contribution to be made by the colony towards the cost of its defences and the maintenance of the Imperial garrison. The Panjdeh Incident and the earlier dispute with Russia in 1876 were simply two war 'scares' that only briefly interrupted the long years of peace which the great nations of Europe enjoyed after the Crimean War. During these years the main aim of the Treasury was to keep the War Office share of the Imperial budget as small as possible. The policy of the government was to maintain the Royal Navy as the principal arm of defence, while the Army was used to garrison the far-flung outposts of Empire. The Royal Navy was to be kept at what was termed the 'two-power standard': in other words, a battleship strength at least equal to the combined strengths of the next two largest navies.

To maintain this standard while keeping the defence budget as small as possible meant that the strength of the Army had to be kept to the minimum necessary to maintain the overseas garrisons. All colonies were therefore expected to make a contribution to the upkeep of the Imperial forces stationed there. The contribution to be made by Singapore had been set in the 1860s, as we have seen, at £50,000 per annum, but in 1889 the basic principle on which a colony's contribution would be based was settled after discussions between the then Chancellor of the Exchequer and the Secretary of State for the Colonies. As a result, it was agreed that the Imperial government would provide the sea defence, that is ships of the Royal Navy, while the colony was to be responsible for its land defences.

As a result of this inter-departmental agreement in London, the contribution to be made by Singapore towards the defence of the colony was raised in 1890 from £50,000 to £100,000 per annum. Needless to say, this doubling of the colony's contribution caused uproar in Singapore, particularly as the Local Defence Committee had stated that it believed that on the outbreak of hostilities between Britain and a major power no co-operation could be expected from the Royal Navy.[6] Indeed, the Colonial Defence Committee in London had itself been somewhat equivocal on the subject, stating that 'the prevention of transportation and landing on British territory of an expedition would depend upon the maintenance of a sufficient naval force in these waters [i.e. the China Seas]'.[7]

The dispute over the colony's contribution to its defence continued throughout the final decade of the nineteenth century. Because of the vehement protests of the colonials the contribution was reduced to £70,000 in 1894, probably as the result of a statistical analysis produced by the Singapore authorities. This showed, according to the 1892–3 Parliamentary returns, that Singapore, with the fourth smallest garrison of all the colonies and the third smallest defence costs, delivered the most money to the Imperial exchequer. However, the contribution was raised to £80,000 in 1895, and by 1898 it had reached £120,000, at which point all the non-official members of the colony's Legislative Council resigned. The matter rumbled on past the turn of the century but was never finally settled to the satisfaction of the colony's taxpayers, largely because the economy of Singapore was booming and the colony was seen by the Imperial government to be rich.

The Imperial policy of keeping Army garrisons as small as possible had its effect on the defence of Singapore. In 1885 the garrison comprised one British infantry battalion, the 1st Battalion the Royal Inniskilling Fusiliers, with a strength of approximately 900 men, together with No 9 Battery of the 1st Brigade, Southern Division, Royal Artillery, with a strength of 100 men.[8] Although a number of gun lascars, that is native gunners, were recruited in order to supplement the Europeans, there were still insufficient gunners to man all the existing guns and provide reliefs.

This situation was partially alleviated by the raising of the Singapore Volunteer Artillery Corps in 1888, with a strength of 100 officers and men recruited from the local European population. The Corps initially comprised a battery of Maxim machine guns purchased by means of local donations, including the outright purchase of one gun by the Sultan of Johore and presented by him to the Corps. The Corps trained at the old Fort Fullerton, and when Fort Palmer was re-armed with breech-loading guns one of the old 7in RML guns from the fort was moved to Fort Fullerton to be used by the Volunteers for training purposes.

There can be no doubt, however, that the size of the garrison was very small when considering the defences that had to be manned. The defence plan at the end of the 1880s envisaged not only an attack on New Harbour, but also one from the mainland to the north. To protect the town of Singapore from such an assault a defensive work known as the Alexandra Position was constructed to the north-west of the city, in order to bar an enemy advance along the Bukit Timah and Alexandra Roads. The position ran for approximately 1,000yds (700m) from Green Hill in the east to Labrador Heights on the coast and comprised barbed wire entanglements supported by infantry redoubts on Labrador Heights, Pine Tree Hill and Green Hill and a battery position for field guns on Pine Tree Hill. The battery position was armed with two 9pdr RML guns, and two 7pdr RML guns armed the

A maxim gun detachment of the Singapore Volunteer Artillery on parade at their drill hall close to the site of the old Fort Fullerton, c. 1882. In the background is the 7in 6.5ton RML gun used for training. (*TNA CO 1069/487*)

redoubts. Two additional 7pdr RML guns were part of the armament of the redoubts on Mount Faber. All these guns were provided from the moveable armament for the general defence of the colony, and manning them placed an additional burden on the gunners of the garrison.

Four more redoubts were built along the Mount Faber ridge; these were the Mount Faber, Spur, Borneo and Guthrie's Hill Redoubts, sited to protect the town from an enemy landing south of the Alexandra Position. A fifth redoubt was also built on the highest point of Blakang Mati.

An additional defensive measure authorized by the War Office was the provision of two submarine minefields for the defence of New Harbour, as previously recommended by Jervois. Submarine mines, or 'torpedoes' as they were originally termed, were first introduced into the British Army in 1872. Seen as a cheap form of harbour defence when compared to the cost of the construction of permanent forts and batteries, submarine minefields used both electro-contact and ground mines laid by specialist companies of the Royal Engineers, who also controlled their firing. Initially, five Royal

Sappers of a Royal Engineers submarine mining company laying a mine. (*Author's collection*)

Engineers submarine mining companies were formed as part of the regular Army, and these were supplemented by a number of volunteer companies at the major mercantile ports in the United Kingdom. Abroad, five locally recruited companies were established, and four of these were based at Far Eastern ports: Singapore, Hong Kong, Colombo and Port Louis in Mauritius.

In 1885 authority was given for the formation of a locally raised submarine mining company of the Royal Engineers in Singapore, to be recruited from indigenous Malays; and the following year twenty-eight 500lb (227kg) ground mines and sixty eight 100lb (45kg) electro-contact mines were dispatched to Singapore.[9] The submarine mining station was to be built on Pulau Brani, but there were delays in establishing the minefields due to difficulties in recruiting Malay personnel. In the end, a composite company was formed of British Royal Engineers personnel and Malays.

The submarine minefields were sited to protect the eastern and western entrances to New Harbour, but these could only form an effective defence if they were covered by the fire of guns, in order to prevent an enemy force lifting and destroying the mines. Approval was given by the War Office for the dispatch of a number of 6pdr QF guns which, together with machine guns, were to form the minefield batteries to be established on Teregeh Point and Tanjong Pagar Spit. In 1890 the battery on Teregeh Point consisted of the two 64pdr RML guns already in place, together with a single Hotchkiss 6pdr QF gun and a Gardner rifle-calibre machine gun. However, the two RML guns were removed in the following year and replaced by an additional 6pdr QF gun. At Tanjong Pagar Spit there were two Gardner rifle-calibre machine guns, but the intention was that these would be replaced by two 6pdr QF guns in due course. In 1889 a total of six Hotchkiss 6pdr QF guns had been delivered to Singapore, and two guns each were deployed at Teregeh Point, Tanjong Pagar Spit and a new position at Berlayer Point on Singapore Island, opposite Fort Siloso. A seventh was retained as a training gun and spare. In 1894 a further two guns were mounted in a battery at Berhala Point on Blakang Mati to defend the entrance to Sinki Strait.

The 6pdr QF gun, made either by Hotchkiss or Nordenfeldt, was installed in ports and harbours to defend the submarine minefields. This example can be seen at Tilbury Fort, on the Thames estuary. (*Author's photograph*)

The position at Berlayer Point was unusual in being sited at the foot of the headland, at beach level. A concrete gun position with four expense ammunition recesses was constructed in the cliff face, accessed by means of three flights of stairs built within the headland. A similar position, known as the Lye Yue Mun Pass Battery, was built for two 6pdr QF guns at Lye Yue Mun Fort in Hongkong. However, it was soon apparent that the Berlayer Point gun position within the cliff face was not ideal, and in 1899 the gun was removed and remounted in a more conventional position within the fort.

By 1890 it was clear that the RML guns were obsolete and to all intents and purposes ineffective. These guns had a low muzzle velocity, reducing their ability to penetrate modern armour, and a slow rate of fire. The 7in 6.5 ton RML gun had a maximum effective range of 1,800yds (1660m) and the 64pdr RML gun even less. The War Office now agreed to remove all the

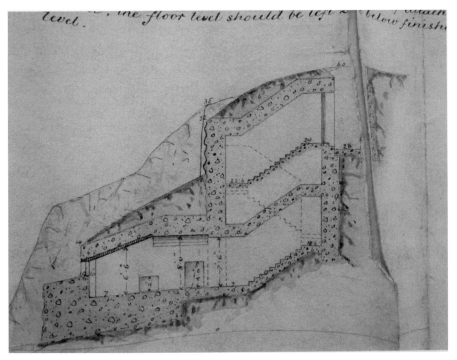

Berlayer Point. The plan clearly shows the unusual siting of the 6pdr QF gun at the bottom of the cliff face. This enabled the gun to cover the submarine minefield with its fire. (*TNA WO 78/3950*)

RML guns in the coastal defence batteries and replace them with modern breech-loaders. The gun selected as a replacement was the new 6in (152mm) QF gun, which came into service in 1894.

This quick-firing gun had a greater effective range than the older Mk IV and Mk VI BL guns and, more importantly, a higher muzzle velocity. The charge for the gun was contained in a brass case rather than in a bag as used in the breech-loaders, and it had a single-motion interrupted screw breech rather than the three-motion mechanism of the earlier 6in BL guns, which permitted a faster rate of fire. This meant that the quick-firing gun was particularly suited for engaging what have been described as 'tip and run' attacks, particularly by heavier warships acting as raiders.

The heavier 9.2in BL Mk IV guns had been installed in Singapore in the mid-1890s and these were mounted in the newly modified Forts Siloso and Pasir Panjang, and in Blakang Mati East Battery. The latter position was renamed Fort Connaught in 1890 after a visit to Singapore by HRH the Duke of Connaught, third son of Queen Victoria.

Further changes to the armament of the defences occurred between 1892 and 1900. The two 10in BL guns for Fort Palmer were finally delivered in 1892 and were mounted in the now totally rebuilt fort. The 10in BL gun positions were constructed within an earth bank, with underground shell and cartridge stores behind each gun. The fort was roughly pentagonal in shape, with a concrete wall extending along three of its sides and acting as

A 10in Mark III BL gun on a Mark I barbette mounting. Two guns of this type and mark were installed in Fort Palmer from 1892 to 1910. The photograph shows a similar mark of gun and mounting at Stonecutters West battery in Hong Kong. (*RAI*)

a scarp to the ditch. The entrance was on the northern side of the fort and here the gorge was open and defended only by a steel 'unclimbable' fence 9½ft (3m) high, backed by a barbed wire fence. In front of No 1 gun there was a single-storey musketry caponier defending the ditch.

However, further bureaucratic wrangling occurred when the War Office requested the use of a site on Mount Wallich, a hill adjacent to Fort Palmer, for the construction of a position-finding cell to control the fire of the new 10in guns. The problem was that the Colonial government was in the progress of demolishing the hill, using the rock in one of Singapore's earliest land reclamation projects, and was not prepared to halt the demolition.[10] Interestingly, the argument advanced by the War Office for a position-finding cell on Mount Wallich was that the effective range of the 10in BL gun when controlled by a position-finder was increased from 4,000 to 10,000yds.

In 1896 new guns were approved for Fort Siloso; this involved the replacement of the two 7in RML guns overlooking New Harbour with two 12pdr QF guns, and two 6in (152mm) QF guns replaced the two 7in RML guns on top of Mount Siloso. However, the 12pdr QF guns were not installed until 1899, and the two 6in (152mm) QF guns were not operational until 1900. In 1897 construction of a new battery at Silingsing Point on Pulau Brani was authorized in order to reinforce the defences of the eastern entrance to New Harbour. This battery was to be armed with two 12pdr QF guns with the role of countering any attempt by enemy torpedo boats to enter New Harbour.

While these improvements in the colony's defences were being approved and installed, one fort was proving to be something of an embarrassment. Fort Tanjong Katong was sited à fleur d'eau, in other words on the beach. Its location was remote, which made it difficult to reinforce should it be attacked; and because of the soft ground on which the fort was built, when the guns were fired the reverberation necessitated the recalibration of the rangefinders after each salvo. As a result, the position was known locally as Fort 'Wash-out'. Added to this, the 8in BL guns were not chasehooped, and one burst when test-fired. The gun was condemned, and orders were given that the others were not to be fired at full charge unless in an emergency, until they had been chasehooped. A new gun was ordered to replace the condemned piece.[11]

So, barely three years after the fort's reconstruction discussions began between the Colonial Defence Committee in London and the colony's Local Defence Committee regarding its efficacy and whether or not it should be abandoned. These discussions continued in a desultory manner until finally, at the turn of the century, the decision was taken to abandon it.

With the turn of the century it could be said that the defences of Singapore were in a reasonable state. However, in Europe political alliances were changing with the rise of Germany. The defeat by Prussia of Austria in 1866 and France in 1870 brought about the unification of Germany and introduced a rising modern and increasingly industrialized power on to the world's stage. Germany was now perceived by the British government to be a greater threat to the United Kingdom than France or Russia, the traditional enemies, as we shall see in the next chapter.

Chapter 6

The First World War: 1900–1920

The turn of the twentieth century saw the first ripples in the placid surface of late Victorian life. Britain was the major world power at this date, with the greatest empire and the largest navy, but was currently involved in a messy war with Boer farmers in South Africa. In the

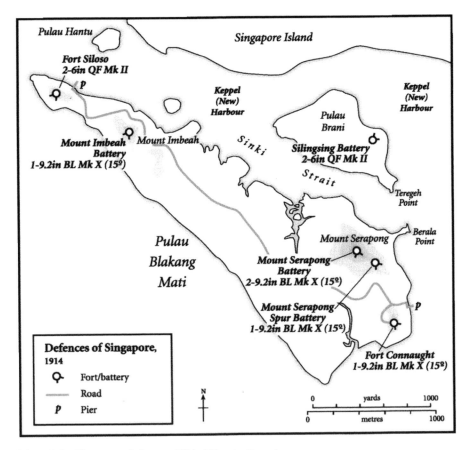

Map of the Singapore defences, 1914. (*Martin Brown*)

Far East, China had recently been defeated in a war with an increasingly industrialized and powerful Japan, while in Europe Britain was forced to reassess its policy towards Germany and its ruler Kaiser Wilhelm II.

In 1902 the Boer War ended, leaving Britain successful in South Africa but without allies in Europe; France, Germany, Austria and Russia had watched Britain's earlier discomfiture against the Boers with considerable pleasure. The British government still believed that Russia posed a threat to India, and so the Foreign Office searched for a potential ally in the Far East who might help to restrain what the Foreign Office saw as Russia's overweening territorial ambitions. After its victory over China in 1895 Japan appeared the most likely candidate, and an Anglo–Japanese Alliance was duly signed in 1902, under the terms of which, by Article 3, each nation promised to support the other if either became involved in war with more than one power. In effect, this relieved the British Admiralty from the necessity of maintaining two-power naval superiority in the Far East.

Two years later Japan was at war with Russia, and by September 1905, after a number of crushing defeats of Russia by Japan, both on land and at sea, a peace treaty was signed at Portsmouth, Maine, at the instigation of President Theodore Roosevelt. Russia's defeat at the hands of an 'Asiatic' nation checked her territorial ambitions to such an extent that Britain no longer considered her to be a threat to India.

Of course, this was to affect the Imperial government's view of the threat to Singapore; but in the interim, in 1901, a further review of the colony's defences had been carried out and the result of this was a recommendation that two 6in (152mm) QF guns should be mounted on Silingsing Point on Pulau Brani. In addition, the construction of four positions for the new coastal defence searchlights, or Defence Electric Lights (DELs) as they were officially termed, was also authorized, in order to cover and illuminate the western and eastern entrances to New Harbour and the minefields. These were concentrated moving lights, and two each were authorized for Teregeh Point and Fort Siloso, together with adjacent observing stations. To man these searchlights half a Fortress Company RE was dispatched to Singapore to reinforce the garrison, which now comprised two battalions of infantry, one British and one Indian. The Royal Artillery garrison now consisted of two companies of the Royal Garrison Artillery, one of which was a company of the Hong Kong-Singapore Battalion, which was formed in 1899.

However, by 1904 it was becoming clear to British policy makers that the major threat to Britain's position as the leading world power was no longer either of Britain's old foes France and Russia, but rather the new player on the world's stage, Germany. Envious of his cousin's empire and determined to make Germany the equal of Britain, the Kaiser initiated a major warship-building programme aimed at equalling the number of battleships in the Royal Navy. The First Navy Law, establishing a six-year programme for the construction of twelve new battleships, had been passed in 1898. In 1900 the Reichstag passed the Second Navy Law, doubling the number of battleships to be built. The naval race between Britain and Germany was well and truly on.

The Owen Committee

In 1905 the Admiralty and the War Office set up a joint committee with instructions 'to report what additions or alterations, if any, are necessary to the existing fixed defences of all defended ports at home to suit modern conditions'.[1] The committee was under the presidency of General J. F. Owen, with four other members, two each from the Army and the Royal Navy. This body, which was to have great influence on future policy concerning fixed defences in the United Kingdom and overseas, was formally known as the Committee on Armaments of Home Ports, but is generally known simply as the Owen Committee.

The committee took as the basis for its consideration the fact that the ports of the United Kingdom might be subjected to three classes of naval attack. These were: Class A – Attack by Battleships; Class B – Attack by Armoured Cruisers; and Class C – Attack by Unarmoured Cruisers, Torpedo Boats or Block Ships. The committee did not consider the threat to overseas ports and coaling stations but it did rationalize the types of armament it considered should be provided to defend ports and harbours against each type of attack. For defence against Class A and Class B attack two types of gun were considered: the 9.2in (233mm) BL gun and the 12in (304mm) BL gun.

By 1905 the latest versions of the 9.2in gun were the marks IX and X, both of which, on a mounting that permitted 15° elevation, fired a shell weighing 380lb (172 kg) to a range of 17,500yds (16,153m). Having considered the two guns, the committee felt that the angles of elevation and descent of shells from each gun did not differ sufficiently to affect long-range shooting, but in barrel life and rapidity of fire the 9.2in gun was greatly superior.[2] In these circumstances, the committee did not believe the mounting of any other kind of gun was necessary in order to deter attack by battleships or armoured cruisers.

The committee then turned its attention to attack by unarmoured ships (Class C). Here the requirement was for rapidity of fire combined with as great a weight of shell as could be provided, and the committee recommended the 6in (152mm) BL Mk VII gun and the 4.7in (120mm) QF Mk V gun as being the most appropriate for this role.

There was no doubt in the minds of the War Office and the Admiralty that the threat to Singapore was unlikely to consist of more than, at most, a single armoured cruiser on a raiding mission. In that circumstance, the latest mark of the 9.2in BL gun was the most suitable for Singapore, particularly as it had a much increased effective range when compared with the range of the older Mk IV guns currently mounted in the Singapore defences.

A further review of the defences was carried out between 1901 and 1906, and as a result of this review a new battery was approved for Pulau Brani, to be sited on the high ground above Silingsing Point. The Silingsing battery was to mount two 6in QF guns, in place of the two 12pdr QF guns currently mounted nearby. These guns had previously been mounted in Fort Connaught in the late 1890s, when the War Office policy of replacing the 7in (177mm) RML guns was implemented.

In 1907, in a further attempt to strengthen its position in Europe vis-à-vis Germany, Britain signed a convention with Russia which clarified the boundaries of each country's respective spheres of influence in Persia, Afghanistan and Tibet. This reduced the potential areas of dispute between the two countries. In 1904 Britain had reached a similar understanding (the Entente Cordiale) with France, who were allied to Russia, and the Anglo-Russian Convention thus led to the establishment of the Triple Entente. This understanding between three great powers eventually became the

A 6in QF Mk II gun in an emplacement at the old Fort Pasir Panjang. The gun is original but is now mounted in one of the gun positions of the later Labrador Battery, in Labrador Park. The gun is of the same type as that mounted at Silingsing Battery. (*Author's photograph*)

basis of the alliance that was to oppose the Central Powers of Germany and Austro-Hungary at the outbreak of war in 1914.

Although the Anglo-Russian Convention reduced even further any threat to Singapore, in 1908 an additional battery was approved for Mount Imbeah on Blakang Mati; this battery was to be part of the re-armament with 9.2in Mk X guns, replacing the older Mk IVs. In 1909 the Mk IV gun mounted in Fort Siloso was removed, and Fort Pasir Panjang and Fort Palmer were disarmed. In addition, the two 6in QF guns mounted in Fort Siloso were moved to a new site, which became the battery for the Western Examination Anchorage to the west of Pulau Blakang Mati. Silingsing was designated the battery for the Eastern Examination Anchorage and was operational in 1910/11. These two batteries supported the Examination Service, which was responsible for controlling and inspecting merchant vessels wishing to enter Singapore in wartime.

The casemates of the old Fort Pasir Panjang in Labrador Park, as they are today. (*Author's photograph*)

By 1913 the operational armament of Singapore had been reduced to six forts and batteries armed with modern guns:

Fort Connaught	1 x 9.2in Mk X BL gun on Mk V 15° mounting.
Mount Imbeah Battery	1 x 9.2in Mk X BL gun on Mk V 15° mounting.
Mount Serapong Spur	1 x 9.2in Mk X BL gun on Mk V 15° mounting.
Mount Serapong	2 x 9.2in Mk X BL guns on Mk V 15° mountings
Fort Siloso	2 x 6in Mk II QF guns on Mk II pedestals
Silingsing Battery	2 x 6in Mk II QF guns on Mk II pedestals

For the general defence of the colony six 6in BL howitzers and twelve 15pdr BLC field guns were provided, and the old 9pdr and 7pdr RML guns were withdrawn. There had also been a substantial increase in the size of the garrison, with the addition of a second company of the Royal Garrison Artillery and the remaining half of the Royal Engineers Fortress company.

However, a major change in the defence of New Harbour had occurred in 1905 with the abolition of submarine mining. This had occurred as a result of intense inter-service rivalry and the acceptance of the primacy of the 'Blue-water School' of defence (belief in the importance of a navy capable of operating across the oceans). There was also the considerable attraction of what were seen as potentially large financial savings, though these proved to be somewhat exaggerated. On 2 December 1904 submarine mining was officially transferred to the Royal Navy, only to be abolished by the Admiralty in the following year. The Royal Navy had always objected to the mining of harbours on the grounds that it curtailed navigation and did not distinguish between friendly and enemy ships, preferring instead to use submarines for harbour defence; so the demise of submarine mining was not unexpected. The result for Singapore was that in 1905 all submarine mines were withdrawn.

In 1913 the Western and Eastern Examination anchorages had been established, the western covered by the guns of Fort Siloso and the eastern by the guns of Silingsing Battery. A further development was the withdrawal of the infantry defences behind King's Hill, so forming a line Bukit Chermin – Keppel Golf Links – Fir Tree Hill – Bell Spur – Ravine Hill – Summit Hill – Mount Faber – Breeze Hill. The new defence line had a depth of 1,500yds (1,385m) at its deepest point.

War

Singapore was something of a backwater during the First World War. In 1914 the garrison comprised the 1st Battalion the King's Own Yorkshire Light Infantry and the 3rd Brahmans, together with 78 Company RGA and 80 Company RGA. However, the King's Own Yorkshire Light Infantry was moved back to the United Kingdom soon after the outbreak of war in August, and seven officers and sixty-three Other Ranks of the Royal Garrison Artillery followed in October, with four 6in BL howitzers and six 15pdr BL field guns from the garrison's moveable artillery. Shortly after the departure of these troops, the 3rd Brahmans returned to India, being replaced by the 5th Light Infantry, another Indian Army regiment.

The 15pdr BLC (breech-loading converted) field gun was the moveable armament of the Singapore forts and batteries prior to the First World War and used to defend these fortifications from landward attack. (*Author's collection*)

The only occasion on which war came to the Straits Settlements was when the German light cruiser SMS *Emden* entered the Bay of Bengal and carried out a number of raids on shipping and coastal installations. On 28 October 1914 SMS *Emden* entered Georgetown Harbour on the island of Penang under false colours. The harbour was undefended as the three 7in and two 64pdr RML guns that had been the armament of Fort Cornwallis had been removed in 1896, but the Russian light cruiser *Zhemchug* was at anchor there. The *Zhemchug* was quickly sunk by torpedoes as was the French destroyer *Mousquet* which, returning from a patrol, gallantly attempted to attack the *Emden* as she left the harbour.

The only other event of note during the war was the mutiny of the 5th Light Infantry, the Indian Army garrison battalion. On 15 February 1915 the battalion was under orders to leave Singapore, but through a failure in communication the sepoys believed that their destination was Mesopotamia rather than their actual posting, Hong Kong. The Muslim sepoys, who comprised about a third of the strength of the battalion, were unhappy at the thought of having to fight the Turks and so become involved in a war against their co-religionists. There had also been considerable unrest in the unit regarding the failure to promote a havildar (sergeant) to the rank of Viceroy's Commissioned Officer. Caught off guard, the garrison suffered casualties as the sepoys rampaged through Singapore, but the mutiny was finally put down by the garrison artillery troops, the Singapore Volunteer Corps and sailors from HMS *Cadmus*. Additional assistance was provided by sailors from Japanese, Russian and French warships, which had hastened to Singapore at the request of the colony's government.

However, there had been serious loss of life: a total of ten British officers and thirty-four other ranks and civilians were killed by the mutineers. These included three officers and two other ranks from the Royal Garrison Artillery, one of whom was serving with the Malay States Guides mountain battery, and two officers and eight other ranks of the Singapore Volunteer Corps, one of whom was a gunner. Some fifty-nine mutineers were killed, and thirty-seven were subsequently tried and executed. During the mutiny Silingsing Battery was held by an officer and fifteen men, while Fort Siloso was manned by a mixed detachment of the Royal Garrison Artillery and the Singapore Volunteer Artillery.

By 1 March the mutiny had been suppressed and steps were taken to reorganize the garrison. The 4th Battalion Shropshire Light Infantry (Territorial Force) arrived from Rangoon to replace the remnants of the mutinous 5th Light Infantry which, in turn, was transferred to the Cameroons; and the Malay States Guides, some Muslim members of which had also been involved in the mutiny, were moved to garrison Aden in September 1915.

As the war in Europe progressed, more and more RGA personnel of the garrison returned to England, their places being taken by permanently mobilized detachments of the Singapore Volunteer Artillery, who manned the examination battery at Fort Siloso, while a number of the Volunteer Engineers assisted in the manning of the Defence Electric Lights.

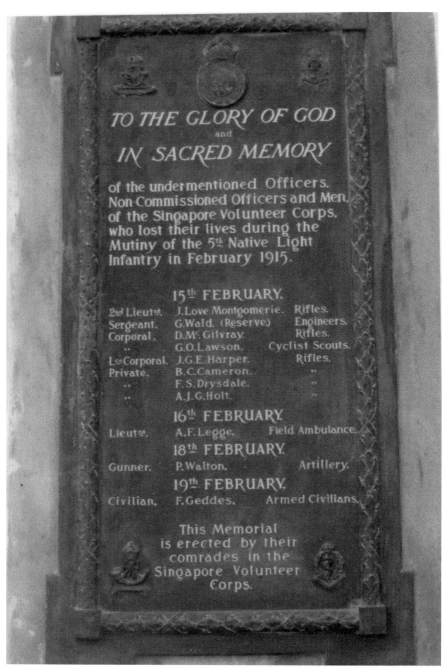

The memorial in St Andrew's Cathedral to the officers and men of the Singapore Volunteer Corps who were killed in the 1915 mutiny of the 5th Light Infantry. (*Author's photograph*)

The Armistice in November 1918 and the advent of peace brought about a return to peacetime establishments and routine, and Singapore continued to be the military backwater it had become in the early years of the century. However, peace had returned to a new world order, and during the war it had become apparent that Japan was now a rising military power in the Far East. Honouring the Anglo-Japanese Treaty, Japan had declared war on Germany on 11 August 1914 and quickly seized the German enclave of Qingdao in north-east China. The Japanese navy, apparently acting almost independently of its government, seized several of Germany's island colonies in the Pacific, the Mariana, Caroline and Marshall Islands.

Throughout the war Japan had an ambivalent attitude to Germany. The Japanese navy had been modelled on and trained by the Royal Navy, but the Japanese army had, in its turn, been modelled on and trained by the Germans, as a result of their overwhelming victories over major European powers in the last half of the nineteenth century. Because the Japanese army was larger than the navy, and in closer contact with the general population, the army's sympathy for Germany, which appeared for some time to be the winning side, considerably influenced the Japanese public.

However, as the war progressed Japan saw its opportunity to gain greater influence and territory in China and also to seize the strategically placed German colonies in the Pacific. The desire to increase its influence in China resulted from Japan's quite inadequate supplies of iron ore, coal, oil and other minerals, all of which were available in China.

Britain gave China an assurance that it was not the Allies' intention to retain the German enclave of Qingdao, and Japan gave China a specific assurance that she had no selfish designs on Chinese territory. As a result, China rejected an offer by Germany to return Qingdao to Chinese sovereignty. Unfortunately for China, Japan's assurances were not to be relied upon, and two months after the fall of Qingdao Japan presented China with what became known as the 'Twenty-one Demands', which were aimed at increasing Japanese influence in China. The Demands were put together in a number of groups, and Group Five demanded the employment by China of Japanese advisers in political, military and financial affairs, and the joint co-ordination of the police departments in important areas. The Twenty-one Demands, if accepted by China, would have given Japan control of the

Chinese army, navy, police and finance; and Japan threatened that if China made the Demands public, even more severe conditions would be applied.

As with most attempts to keep any treaty secret, details of the Twenty-one Demands quickly began to leak out, and British diplomatic pressure was brought to bear in order to persuade Japan to drop them. This pressure, in turn, resulted in a reduction of British popularity in Japan and a loss of British influence with the Japanese government. Despite this, the Japanese, albeit reluctantly, continued to support the Allies in the war against Germany and even dispatched warships to the Mediterranean to assist in protecting convoys, so releasing Royal Navy and French warships for other duties.

So the stage was now set for the rise of Japan as a world power, primarily at the expense of Britain and France.

Chapter 7

Building the Base: 1921–1939

With the signing of the peace treaty at the end of the First World War in 1919 and the scuttling of the German High Seas Fleet at Scapa Flow in the same year, the Royal Navy remained the largest navy in the world. However, the increase in size of the United States and Japanese navies during the war, together with the acute post-war financial crisis facing Britain, meant that it was no longer possible for the Royal Navy to maintain its pre-war 'two power' standard. The increase in the size of the Japanese navy, in particular, appeared to the British government to pose a threat to Britain's sea communications with India, Australia, and New Zealand.

If, as was clear, the Royal Navy could not maintain a substantial fleet in the Far East, then at the very least it must be able to dispatch a fleet to protect Britain's eastern possessions and aid the Australian and New Zealand navies, should that become necessary. However, any such fleet dispatched to the Far East could only operate successfully if it was provided with base facilities, including dry docks, wharves, workshops, storehouses and fuel depots; and in 1919 no such base existed east of Suez.

The fact that it was no longer possible to maintain fleets in home waters and in the Mediterranean and the Far East at the same time was reinforced by the belief that it no longer appeared necessary to do so. In 1919 a war-weary British government instructed the armed forces to draft their future budget estimates on the assumption that the British Empire would not be engaged in any major war during the next ten years.

So the British fleet was to be held centrally in European waters, with an ability to reinforce the Far East as and when necessary; but, as previously noted, this policy required a naval base with full facilities for maintaining a fleet. Where was such a base to be sited?

Four possible harbours suggested themselves: Colombo in Ceylon (Sri Lanka), Sydney in Australia, Hong Kong and Singapore. Colombo was quickly dismissed as being too far from any foreseeable area of operations, and Hong Kong was considered to be too close to Japanese airfields on Formosa (Taiwan). The choice then lay between Sydney and Singapore. After considering both cities, the Committee of Imperial Defence ruled against Sydney on the grounds that the Australian harbour was too far from the Malayan Peninsula and Hong Kong to be an effective base if the reinforcing fleet was faced, as seemed most likely, with a hostile Japan.

At its meeting on 16 June 1921 the British Cabinet accepted the Committee of Imperial Defence's recommendation that Singapore be developed into a naval base sufficient in size to support the main fleet which would be sent in the event of war in the Pacific. In addressing the cabinet, Arthur Balfour, the President of the Council, said:

> We have come to the conclusion that one of the most pressing needs for Imperial defence is that Singapore should be made into a place where the British Fleet can concentrate for the defence of the Empire, of our interest in the East, our interests in India, our interests in the smaller possessions there, and that for that purpose it is absolutely necessary to undertake works at Singapore. Those works cannot be finished in a day. They cannot be finished in a year. They must take some time to complete'.[1]

So the British government became committed to the construction of a major naval base in the Far East, despite the fact that at this time the great nations of the world were considering seriously the matter of disarmament.

At the end of the First World War the three major Allied naval powers, Great Britain, the United States and Japan, each had a major naval building programme in hand. The United States Navy planned the construction of a fleet of fifty modern battleships, with six battleships and six battlecruisers presently under construction; the Japanese planned to build eight battleships and eight battlecruisers; while the British naval estimates for 1921 included funds for the construction of four battleships and four battlecruisers, with four more battleships in the following year.

The Japanese battleship *Nagato*. Armed with eight 16in guns, this was one of the battleships that the provision of 15in coast defence guns for Singapore was designed to counter. (*Author's collection*)

Exhausted financially, Britain could not afford another arms race akin to that before the war, while the American public also had no appetite for President Wilson's naval expansion programme. So the political stage was set for a naval disarmament conference, which the newly elected President Harding's administration suddenly called in Washington in November 1921.

For Great Britain the conference was to have disastrous consequences, since of the three main powers, Britain, the United States and Japan, only Britain had a worldwide empire to defend. The conference resulted in the Washington Naval Treaty, which limited both the tonnage and the construction of capital ships and aircraft carriers, and also included limits on the size of other warships. Under the terms of the treaty, battleships and battlecruisers were to be limited to a standard displacement of 35,000 tons, with guns of no larger calibre than 16in (406mm). Aircraft carriers were to be limited to a maximum displacement of 27,000 tons, and the limit for cruisers was set at 10,000 tons.

The ratio of permitted naval forces was set as follows:

Great Britain and the United States	5
Japan	3
France and Italy	1.75

In overall tonnage terms this worked out at:

Great Britain and the United States	525,000 tons
Japan	315,000 tons
France and Italy	175,000 tons

The treaty also specified which capital ships should be scrapped and when the remaining ships could be replaced. This resulted in the United States having to scrap thirty existing or planned battleships, Britain scrapping twenty-three and Japan seventeen. A further result was the feeling in Japan that the treaty was unfair: because of its lack of parity in tonnage ratio, Japan had once again been apparently snubbed by the Western powers.

For Britain the effects of the treaty were twofold – a reduction in warships, followed by a reduction in personnel in the Royal Navy and the Army. In fact, the overall budget for the armed forces was reduced by 42 per cent under what was known as the 'Geddes Axe', the reductions having been recommended by the newly established Committee on National Expenditure, chaired by Sir Eric Geddes, previously First Lord of the Admiralty. However, although it was agreed that there should be no new military bases in the Pacific region, this did not affect the construction of the naval base at Singapore.

The question now was where the new base should be built. A number of sites were suggested and considered, including the anchorage of Selat Suiki, some miles south-west of Singapore Island, Keppel Harbour and the Strait of Johore (also known as Old Strait) at the northern tip of Singapore Island. Serious consideration was given to the selection of the Selat Suiki Roads, but on investigation it was decided that its exposed situation meant that ships anchored there would be vulnerable to attack both by aircraft and submarines. In order to protect the anchorage it was estimated that an eleven mile-long breakwater would be needed at the enormous cost of £20 million. To this sum would have to be added the cost of constructing all the ancillary buildings and docks, thus effectively ruling out the anchorage as a possible site.

Keppel Harbour, which was favoured by a number of senior Royal Navy officers, was now a busy commercial anchorage, and Singapore Town had expanded along the shore of the harbour, making the land needed for the

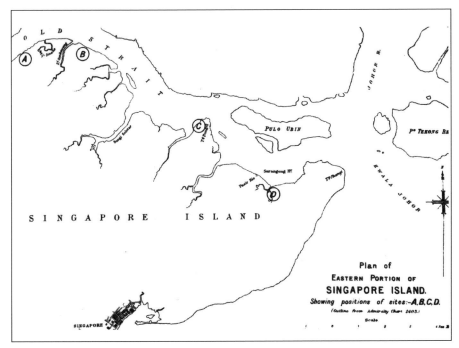

The map shows the four locations originally considered as possible sites for the new naval base: **A** Sungei Senoko, **B** Sembawang, **C** Pungol, **D** Tampines. (*Author's collection*)

base either unavailable or too expensive. That left only the anchorage in the Johore Strait as a suitable location.

It appeared to the officers carrying out the evaluation that in the area of the Johore Strait there was a reasonable depth of water, provided some dredging was carried out, and space for twenty capital ships to anchor. The problem was, however, that a road and rail causeway between Woodlands on the north of Singapore Island and the town of Johore Bahru on the mainland of peninsular Malaya had been planned and was in the course of construction. This would be a permanent structure and would block the strait once completed, so limiting the space available for the new base to the area east of the causeway.

Four sites on the shore of the strait were considered before the decision was taken to construct the new base at Sungei Sembawang. The other three sites were Sungei Senoko, Punggol and Tampines. Senoko was quickly dismissed because of its high foreshore, while a base at Punggol would have required massive land reclamation, and Tampines was considered too vulnerable to attack. That left only the Sembawang district, which was chosen on the principle that it had more advantages than disadvantages, rather than because it was the ideal location.

The construction of the base at Sembawang involved the re-routing of the Sungei Sembawang, a small river that entered the Strait of Johore at the proposed site, together with the reclamation of a considerable amount of mangrove swamp. Despite these drawbacks, by the end of 1922 the site at Sembawang had been approved by the Committee of Imperial Defence, although the War Office expressed the view that in order to protect the new base from enemy artillery fire a 30-mile (48km) defensive perimeter would be required on the mainland. In 1923 plans to build the new base were formally announced, and the Colonial Defence Committee proposed the following fixed defences:

2 x 15in (380mm) BL guns at the eastern end of Singapore Island south-west of Tanjong Changi.

2 x 15in BL guns west of Singapore town at Pasir Panjang.

2 x 9.2in (233mm) BL guns on 45° mountings at the west entrance to Old (Johore) Strait.

2 x 9.2in BL guns on 15° mountings on Pulau Blakang Mati.

2 x 9.2in BL guns on 45° mountings at the east entrance to Old (Johore) Strait.

2 x 6in (152mm) BL guns on either side of the channel to the western end of Pulau Tekong Besar.

2 x 4.7in (120mm) QF guns on Singapore island to cover the eastern channel.

In addition, the four 6in QF guns already in place for the defence of Keppel Harbour were to be retained, together with the two similar calibre guns on the western side of Singapore Island.

The initial Admiralty plans were for a base capable of supporting a fleet of at least seven battleships and ancillary vessels. This would entail the construction of at least ten docks, with workshops; nearly 2 miles (3km) of wharves; a huge inner basin that could be sealed by locks themselves capable of forming additional graving docks; a floating dock; and a storage area capable of holding the fuel requirements of the fleet. To this had to be added accommodation blocks, married quarters and a hospital, together with a seaplane base. This plan was known as the 'Green Scheme', but in the post-war economic climate it failed to gain acceptance by the Treasury, and the Admiralty was forced to scale down its ambitions.

The new and much reduced plan, known as the 'Red Scheme', was based on a much smaller fleet being sent to Singapore. This plan retained only a single graving dock and a floating dock, with less than half the number of wharves originally proposed and with reductions in all other areas of the original 'Green Scheme'. Even this new scheme was estimated to cost in the region of £15 million, without taking into account the cost of the defences and the fuel required to maintain the fleet.

Notwithstanding the selection of the base location and its proposed armament, work on building the base did not proceed smoothly. In January 1924 the first ever British Labour government came to power, with Ramsay Macdonald as Prime Minister. On 17 March 1924 the new government decided to abandon construction of the base, Macdonald describing the project as 'a wild and wanton scheme'. However, the Labour government fell in November of the same year, and a Conservative government under Stanley Baldwin returned to power. The Conservatives quickly reversed the decision to cancel construction of the base, but work proceeded relatively slowly.

Under the policy of 'no war for ten years' the next significant date would be 1929, when the ten years were up. However, on the world political scene disarmament was very much in the air, and on 27 August 1928 the Kellogg-Briand Pact, or the 'General Treaty for the Renunciation of War as an Instrument of National Policy' as it was formally titled, was signed. The original signatories were Germany, France and the United States, and most other nations signed soon after.

The hope that all would disarm came at a time when the world was about to face probably the greatest financial crisis it had ever seen till then. In June 1929 the Conservative Party lost the general election to Ramsay Macdonald's Labour Party, which gained the most seats in the House of Commons but failed to win an overall majority. The balance of power in the Commons was now held by Lloyd George's Liberals.

In October 1929 there occurred the Wall Street financial 'crash', followed quickly by a similar fall on the London Stock Exchange. The new Labour government, faced with a worldwide financial collapse, took the opportunity in 1930 to convene the London Naval Disarmament Conference, while at the same time ordering work on the defences of Singapore to be suspended and work on the naval base to be slowed down. At the conference, the British delegation, believing that there was no likelihood of war in the immediate future and bearing in mind the recent Kellogg-Briand Pact, offered to reduce the number of cruisers in the Royal Navy and suspend work on the Singapore base. The result of the conference was the Treaty for the Limitation and Reduction of Naval Armament, known as the London Naval Treaty, signed on 22 April 1930 by the representatives of Great Britain, France, Italy, Japan and the United States.

The treaty placed a limit on the numbers of heavy cruisers in each navy and restricted the displacement tonnage and gun calibres of submarines. In addition, the British government followed up on its offer and suspended work on the Singapore base as a gesture towards general disarmament. However, prior to the suspension of work, a massive floating dock, the third largest in the world at that time with a lift of 50,000 tons, had been ordered from the British shipbuilders Swan Hunter on Tyneside and was delivered in 1929.

The Japanese had been badly hit by the financial cataclysm that struck their economy after the American stock market crash. The value of the yen plummeted, driving Japan off the gold standard, and the market for silk, Japan's main export, dried up, ruining millions of small farmers. In addition, high tariff barriers erected by the western nations caused the market for Japanese manufactured goods to vanish.

The impact of the Great Depression forced Japan to look towards China, where the country already had huge economic and industrial interests. However, the Japanese in Manchuria faced the growing threat of Chinese resurgent nationalism in the shape of General Chiang Kai-shek and his Kuomintang government and army. Acting almost independently of the Japanese government, the Japanese Kwantung Army in Manchuria staged a number of 'incidents' aimed at providing suitable excuses for a takeover of the commodity-rich province of Manchuria.

In September 1931 elements of the Japanese army engineered such an incident in Manchuria by exploding a device on the South Manchuria Railway. Although there were no injuries to passengers or railway staff, the Japanese government blamed the incident on the Chinese warlord Marshall Zhang Xueliang. In March 1932, using the incident as an excuse, the Japanese army occupied the city of Mukden and the mineral-rich provinces of north-eastern China, renaming the area Manchukuo and installing the former emperor of China, Puyi, as titular head of the puppet state.

In fact, there was a brief Sino–Japanese war as the Japanese followed up the Mukden 'incident' with the Shanghai 'incident' in January 1932. The latter arose from an attack on five Japanese Buddhist monks that escalated

The opening of the King George VI graving dock on 14 February 1938. The photograph shows the Governor of the Straits Settlements, Sir Shenton Thomas, aboard his yacht *Seabelle II*, breaking the ribbon. (*TNA ADM 116/3664*)

One of the two 9.2in Mark X BL guns on a Mark V barbette mounting at Mount Serapong battery in 1935. The photograph shows the gun crew at action stations. (*Courtesy of Sentosa Leisure Group*)

into serious rioting and an upsurge of anti-Japanese and anti-Imperialist protests in the Chinese city and the International Concessions. The Japanese government deployed troops, ships and aircraft to Shanghai and demanded compensation for the damage caused to Japanese property. The incident might have been settled without serious conflict had not aircraft from a Japanese aircraft carrier bombed the Chinese quarter of Shanghai. Japanese forces occupied areas of the city, only to be faced by the Kwantung 19th Route Army. Fighting broke out between the Japanese army and the 19th Route Army, which was reinforced by Chiang Kai-shek's 5th Army, and continued until 2 March.

The Japanese occupation of Manchuria was roundly condemned at the League of Nations in Geneva by all the major powers. The League dispatched a commission to report on the problem and, meanwhile, called on Japan to withdraw from Manchuria while the commission investigated. Japan refused to withdraw its troops, and when the commission reported in October 1932 it stated that Japan should withdraw from Manchuria. Having considered the report, the Assembly of the League held a vote on the issue in February 1933 and accepted the report by a majority of forty-two to one (Japan). The immediate result was that Japan withdrew from the League of Nations, the first major world power to do so.

The Japanese actions in China and its formal renunciation of the Washington Naval Treaty in 1934 were clear indications to the British government that Japan now posed a major threat to British interests in the Far East. It was obvious, therefore, that the construction of the base at Singapore was now a matter of the first importance. Consequently, there was a formal Cabinet decision to resume work on the naval base, and installation of the armament for the base was authorized.[2]

The planned completion date for the naval base was set at 1937 although, as with most major building projects, this target date was not met, and it was not until the following year that the King George VI graving dock was opened, with considerable pomp and ceremony. At more than 975ft (300m) in length, it was the largest dry dock in the world at that time and capable of taking HMS *Hood*, the largest Royal Navy capital ship. In addition, a second floating dock was purchased from the Dutch authorities in Java. This had a lift capacity of 5,000 tons and could take vessels up to 350ft (107m) in length.

By 1939 the naval base was operational, but it was not until 1941 that the workshops, barracks and other facilities, extending over an area of some 21 square miles (5,698h), were finally completed, at the enormous cost of £60 million.

Chapter 8

Arming the Base: 1923–1933

No war for ten years

O nce the initial decision to construct the naval base had been taken, the next consideration was how it should be defended. In 1905 the recommendation of the Owen Committee, that the main counter-bombardment coastal defence gun should have a calibre of 9.2in (233mm), had been accepted, but by 1921 the factors affecting that recommendation had changed. The standard Mark V mounting for the 9.2in Mark X BL gun permitted a maximum elevation of 15°, giving a maximum range of 21,000yds (19,385m). However, a new mounting, the Mk VII, permitted firing at an angle of 35°, which increased the maximum range of the gun

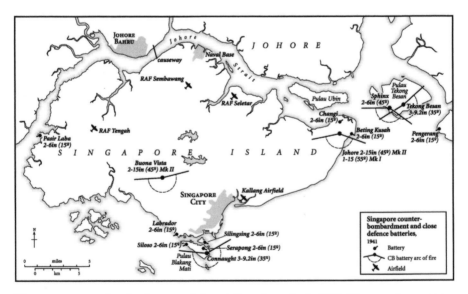

Singapore counter-bombardment and close defence batteries in 1937. The map shows all the batteries completed or under construction. (*Martin Brown*)

to 29,000yds (26,770m). In European and Atlantic waters the Admiralty's belief was that the Royal Navy would not face an enemy fleet equipped with modern battleships, but in the Far East it would be a different matter. It was now appearing increasingly likely that Japan was a potential enemy. This undoubtedly influenced the Oversea Defence Committee's recommendation that four 15in (380mm) BL guns be installed to defend Singapore, the first guns of this calibre to be proposed for use in a coastal defence role by the British Army.

The permitted increase in the calibre of battleship armament to 16in (403mm) under the Washington Naval Treaty, together with the fact that the Admiralty had now set a period of forty-two days as being the minimum time before a British fleet could reach Singapore, reinforced the need for larger calibre guns in coastal defence. This was because it was clear that before the fleet could reach Singapore the colony could be faced with attack by Japanese battleships armed with 16in guns.

Although in 1923 the Oversea Defence Committee had made comprehensive suggestions for the armament of the base, it would be some considerable time before the numbers and types of guns would be decided or, indeed, whether guns would form the primary means of defence,.

In 1923 the Admiralty submitted a memorandum to the Committee of Imperial Defence stating that in the naval view an armament of four 15in guns was inadequate to repel an attack on Singapore by a fleet of six battleships, the total number of such ships in the Japanese fleet at that date. The Admiralty believed that to provide an appropriate deterrent four such guns would be needed in the eastern part of the island, with two additional guns sited in the west.

The following year, 1924, the Air Ministry put forward their objection to any heavy fixed armament being provided for Singapore. In the view of the Air Staff it was vital to maintain the RAF as an independent air arm, and in order to ensure this position it was necessary that the RAF should find one or more peacetime roles. The defence of the new base at Singapore appeared to be one such role.

The Army and the Royal Navy were not prepared to accept that guns should be replaced by aircraft, particularly as the aircraft suitable for an anti-shipping role was still in the course of development. The plane offered

The Hawker Horsley single-engined biplane bomber was the aircraft the Air Ministry planned to develop as a torpedo-bomber (*Author's collection*)

by the Air Ministry was the Hawker Horsley, which eventually entered service in Singapore in 1930.

Unprepared to accept this delay, both the Army and the Admiralty vigorously opposed the Air Ministry's proposal, though the Army authorities did agree that a number of spotting aircraft would be required because of the vastly increased ranges at which the 15in guns could engage targets. Cancellation of the Singapore base project by the newly elected Labour government brought the debate to a temporary close.

With the return of the Conservative Party to power at the end of 1924, and the re-activation of the Singapore project, the aircraft versus guns debate was renewed. In January 1925 a special Singapore sub-committee of the Committee of Imperial Defence was set up. The remit of this committee was:

To examine the sites [in Singapore] approved by the CID on 14 December 1922 for the naval base, aerodrome and seaplane station.

To consider the rate at which the naval base and the defences necessary for its protection should be proceeded with.

To consider the programme of construction to be aimed at both for the naval base and the defences including examination of the deterrents as alternatives to heavy guns against attack by capital ships.

This high-powered committee was chaired by Lord Curzon, the Lord President of the Council, together with the Chancellor of the Exchequer, Winston Churchill, the Secretaries of State for War and Air, the First Lord of the Admiralty, the First Sea Lord, the Chief of the General Staff and the Chief of the Air Staff.[1] In all, the committee held eight meetings between January 1925 and October 1928.

The Chief of the Air Staff, Air Chief Marshal Sir Hugh Trenchard, submitted a scheme for replacing the heavy armament at Singapore with torpedo bombers. Trenchard argued that air power was cheaper, more mobile and had a longer range than guns; also that the Japanese fleet would be vulnerable to air attack. He offered a fighter squadron, two squadrons of torpedo bombers and a flight of seaplanes to provide the long-range defence of the base, though only the seaplanes were to be permanently stationed in Singapore. This rather pitiful allocation of aircraft to the defence of the island gives a clear indication of the underestimation of the Japanese navy at this time. As a result, a technical sub-committee of the Oversea Defence Committee was established to investigate the whole subject of ships versus shore guns; but, in fact, only one meeting of this sub-committee was ever held.[2]

The War Office and the Admiralty remained deadlocked in their discussions with the Air Ministry until May 1925. The Chief of the Imperial General Staff pointed out that the aircraft proposed for the defence of Singapore would not be stationed there, so would provide no deterrent, and the First Sea Lord, Admiral of the Fleet Lord Beatty, forcefully supported the installation of 15in guns.

In the end, in July 1925 the Chief of the Air Staff reluctantly agreed that the armament proposed by the Oversea Defence Committee in 1923 would provide an adequate deterrent. However, he maintained his view that a force of aircraft would provide equally efficient protection at less cost.[3] In a resulting compromise, it was agreed that three 15in guns would be mounted as part of the first stage of arming the Singapore base, but before a second stage was implemented there was to be a fresh investigation into the comparative efficiency and economy of guns when compared with aircraft.

In October 1925 the Singapore sub-committee accepted the proposals for the medium, light and anti-aircraft defences, but instructed the Air Staff to produce in greater detail their scheme for aircraft to replace the heavy armament. Some minor changes to the original proposals were accepted, with the reduction of two 4.7in (120mm) QF guns, an increase of two 6in (152mm) BL guns (to be installed at Changi Point) and the substitution of eight Twin 6pdr QF equipments for the original proposal of eighteen 2pdr Pompoms as the anti-coastal motor boat armament. The newly developed Twin 6pdr QF equipments had a rate of fire, with a well-trained gun crew, of 120 rounds per minute, and outperformed the older 2pdr Pompom in both rate of fire and weight of shell.

At this meeting the General Staff presented their views on the possibility of attack from the north in a memorandum on the defence of the base:

> The General Staff are therefore of the opinion that the danger of the Northern Site for the Naval base being captured or destroyed by land attack through Johore is remote. In fact, as a result of their considerations, they conclude that a direct attack on the Island of Singapore itself is more likely to be attempted by an enemy than a landing in Johore North of the Old [Johore] Strait. Coastal reconnaissance indicates that the most suitable area for such a hostile landing would be on the South of Singapore Island, in the vicinity of Keppel Harbour. Against such a attack, therefore, the Northern Site would be less exposed.[4]

The following year, 1926, three 15in Mark I BL guns were formally approved for the defence of Singapore, two to be installed at Bee Hoe, close to the 13th milestone on the old Changi road, and the third on Blakang Mati. These guns fired a shell weighing 1,938lb (879kg) and, at an elevation of 45°, had a maximum range of 42,000yds (38,770m); however, limitations in range-finding reduced their practical range to around 36,000yds (33,230m).

A Twin 6pdr QF equipment, similar to the guns provided for the defence of Singapore, to be seen at the Forte do Bom Sucesso in Lisbon, Portugal. (*Author's photograph*)

Before any further large-calibre guns were authorized, there was to be a re-examination of the whole matter, which 'shall include a fresh investigation un-prejudiced by the present agreement, of the question of the substitution of aircraft for the balance of the 15in guns in the light of air development during the intervening period'.[5] It would seem that, in 1926, there was still no suitable torpedo bomber in the RAF inventory, and the Committee of Imperial Defence believed that it would be a further four years before suitable aircraft could be developed.

The Singapore sub-committee, having accepted the view of both the Admiralty and the War Office that the gun should retain its place as the main deterrent against naval attack, also accepted the War Office recommendations for the armament of the base. The War Office's proposed armament was now:

6 x 15in BL guns
4 x 9.2in BL guns on high-angle 55° mountings
2 x 9.2in BL guns on 35° mountings
4 x 6in BL guns on high-angle 75° mountings
10 x 6in BL guns on 15° mountings
8 x Twin 6pdr QF equipments

The heavy armament was to be mounted in two stages, with three guns in the first stage and three more in the second. Three 15in BL gun mountings were to be ordered for the guns of the first stage, with one mounting to be complete by 1932. The Royal Navy was to provide the guns from its reserve stocks.

The Sub-Committee considered the possibility of an attack on Singapore from the north, but came to the same conclusion as the General Staff that such an attack was unlikely in view of the nature of the country north of the Strait of Johore. An attack by what was termed coastal motor boats was also considered unlikely, and the installation of the eight Twin 6pdr QF equipments for defence against such an attack, which had previously been approved, was postponed.

In addition to the surface armament, a decision was made to provide the base with suitable anti-aircraft defences. Two 3in (76mm) 20cwt semi-mobile AA guns had already been dispatched to Singapore, and a further twenty-two were now authorized.

The focus of the defences of Singapore had shifted from New Harbour, now re-named Keppel Harbour, to the eastern entrance to the Strait of Johore, in order to provide protection for the naval base. It was accepted that for protection against battleship attack the garrison would have to rely on the three 15in BL guns to be installed in the first stage of the re-armament of the island. A site was selected for one gun at Bee Hoe plantation, with a second at Mata Ikan, south-east of the 10th Milestone. The third gun was to be mounted on Blakang Mati. The Bee Hoe and Mata Ikan guns were to cover the water south-east of Singapore Town up to a distance of 35,000yds (33,307m), while the Blakang Mati gun was to cover the water south and west of Singapore Town out to a similar distance, except for a small area near Tanjong Bukas.

In addition, the older 9.2in BL guns were to be removed and the Mark X guns installed on more modern mountings, also to defend the Strait of Johore. Two new batteries were proposed, one for Pengerang Ridge on the Johore mainland to the east, and the other for Tanjong Gul on the west of Singapore Island. The War Office also proposed the installation of twelve additional 6in BL guns in six batteries, making a total of sixteen such guns. The batteries at Fort Siloso and Silingsing were to be retained for the defence

The photograph shows the two 6in Mk VII close defence guns of Labrador Battery before the overhead cover was added. (*TNA WO 252/1359*)

of Keppel Harbour, while new batteries were to be located at Pengelih Point at Pengerang; Pulau Tekong Besar; Pulau Tekong Kechil; Changi Point; and Pulau Ubin. These latter five batteries were all sited to defend the eastern entrance to the Strait of Johore. For the defence of the western entrance to the Strait a sixth battery of two 6in guns was to be sited at Pasir Laba.

According to the War Office proposal, a number of the new guns were to be installed on new high-angle mountings that had still to be developed. Some of the 9.2in guns were to have 55° mountings, while the 6in guns were to be on mountings giving them an elevation of 70° (reduced from the originally proposed 75°); this would give them a dual coastal defence and anti-aircraft role.

The Gillman Commission

Having decided on the appropriate armament for the defences of the colony, in 1927 the War Office decided to send a commission to Singapore headed by

Lieutenant General Sir Webb Gillman, the Director of the Royal Artillery, with instructions to inspect and make recommendations for both the number and the location of the fixed defence batteries. The Gillman Commission was hampered in its mission by the unwillingness of the colony's governor, Sir Hugh Clifford, to make land available for military purposes unless he was assured that no part of the cost of the defences would fall on the local community. This divergence of opinion delayed the planning of the layout of the defences and the necessary barracks for the troops manning the fixed defences.

The Gillman Commission reported in early 1928 and, despite the fact that the land required for the batteries had still not been agreed, produced recommendations which differed quite markedly from the original War Office plan. These included the proposal that two 15in guns should be installed at Bee Hoe and two more at Blakang Mati. A further recommendation of the Commission was that rather than siting two 9.2in guns on Pengerang Ridge, on the Johore mainland, as the War Office had proposed, no guns should be sited there, only an observation post.

In the view of the Commission it was appropriate that the majority of the 6in guns should be sited to defend the eastern entrance to the Strait of Johore, and the Commission agreed with the War Office that batteries should be installed on the islands of Pulau Tekong Besar, Pulau Tekong Kechil, and Pulau Ubin. Added to these, two 6in BL guns on 70° mountings were to be installed at Changi Point. However, the Commission appears not to have been concerned that three of the new batteries were to be sited on undeveloped islands, each some considerable distance from Singapore town, although the new naval base, when constructed, would be reasonably close. Nevertheless, the troops manning the batteries would be isolated and would have to be transported and re-supplied by boat.

The Commission, however, did not recommend a 6in battery at Pengerang. The original requirement for a battery in this location was to block the Calder Passage, a narrow strait between Pulau Tekong Besar and the Johore mainland. The general view expressed to the Commission was that the passage was too narrow and shallow for large vessels to navigate, and the Admiralty planned to block it with an anti-coastal motor boat (AMTB) boom. In these circumstances the Commission dismissed the need for the proposed battery at Pengelih Point. The Chiefs of Staff endorsed this recommendation but, as we shall see, this decision was based on a false assumption, since the passage was indeed navigable to ships as large as destroyers.

It would appear that the decision to postpone the installation of anti-coastal motor boat (AMTB) guns had now been reversed, as the Commission recommended a number of positions for these guns on the same islands as the 6in batteries, together with ten Defence Electric Lights (DELs). Four of these lights were to be installed on Pulau Tekong Besar; a further two at Java Point on Pulau Ubin; and two more at Changi Point on Singapore Island. Two additional lights were recommended for either Balai Point on Pulau Ubin or the Government Bungalow site at Changi. Six of these were to be concentrated beam (fighting lights) together with two dispersed beam (observation) lights. The decision on the remaining two lights, whether they would be concentrated or dispersed beam, was to depend on whether the site chosen for them was Pulau Ubin or Changi.

The bulk of the Commission's recommendations concerned the eastern and central areas of Singapore Island, but when General Gillman came to consider the western defences he made no recommendations. The War Office had planned to site a new two-gun 9.2in battery at Tanjong Gul, and two 6in BL guns at Pasir Laba; but Gillman believed that the whole question of the defence of the western area required reconsideration.

On the subject of fire control, however, the Commission appears to have accepted the War Office plan that there should be two Fortress Observation Posts, one consisting of six position-finding cells on Mount Faber, and the other, comprising two cells, on Point 270 on the Pasir Panjang ridge.

New guns for old

By 1928 it would seem that the War Office was having doubts about the efficacy of the existing coastal defence guns in its armoury. The techniques by which field artillery engaged targets concealed from ground observation had made rapid progress as a result of experience in the First World War. Where coastal artillery was concerned, however, methods of engaging targets had not improved since the beginning of the century. Nor, indeed, had there been improvements in the range at which coastal artillery could engage targets. As we have seen, there were currently proposals for a 55° mounting on the 9.2in BL gun and a 70° mounting on the 6in BL gun, but both these had still to be developed.

The War Office, therefore, decided to conduct trials using the current 9.2in BL guns at Malta and Portsmouth in order to gauge the efficacy of the gun when engaging a target screened by smoke, and against the target ship HMS *Centurion* using all forms of observation, including aircraft and a kite balloon.

The results of the trials showed that spotting by aircraft was essential for successful counter-bombardment shooting by coastal defence guns; also that, in order to overcome the difficulty of the 'zone of dispersion' of the gun and so assist in ranging, the number of shells projected against the target during the comparatively short time it would be within range needed to be increased. The War Office Standing Committee on Coast Defence stated in their report that to sink a ship would require salvos of at least four rounds at intervals of not less than twenty seconds. The committee therefore recommended that all areas from where long-range bombardment was possible should be covered by fire units of at least four guns each.[6]

The committee made the point that it would be premature to proceed with the 55° mounting for the 9.2in BL gun in the light of the decision by the Singapore sub-committee of the Chiefs of Staff Committee to modify the existing Mark V 15° mounting to enable the gun to attain an elevation of 35° for use in Singapore. This meant that the expensive development of a new mounting could, for the moment, be postponed.

The new 35° mounting (to be known as the Mark VII) for the 9.2in BL gun would provide it with a range of 25,000yds (23,076m), which was eventually increased to 29,600yds (27,323m). The new mounting was provided with hydraulic elevation and traverse, together with a hydraulic rammer. These improvements increased considerably the rate of fire of the gun and made manning it less physically demanding.

Development of a 70° mounting for the 6in BL gun appears also to have been put on hold at this time, though an experimental 75° mounting was noted as being under construction at the Royal Artillery Proof and Experimental Establishment at Shoeburyness in Essex. Subsequently, however, a new 45°

mounting was developed shortly before the outbreak of war in 1939 for the new 6in Mk XXIV BL gun.

The Cabinet Sub-Committee on Coast Defence having now formally decreed that the gun should retain its place as the main deterrent against naval attack, the Chiefs of Staff Committee agreed that the first three 15in guns should be completed within five years but the second stage would be postponed. Authority was given for the construction of three mountings for the three heavy guns, with one mounting to be completed by 1932. The Royal Navy was to provide the guns from their reserve stocks. However, the committee, noting the result of the recent Malta and Portsmouth trials, which had shown that for maximum effect it was necessary to group artillery in four-gun batteries, recommended that the proposed plan for the siting of the three guns should be altered; the guns should instead be installed in one three-gun battery or, rather strangely, possibly in two batteries: one two-gun battery and one single-gun battery.

In 1930, with the economy in free fall as a result of the Wall Street Crash, the newly elected Labour government took the decision to suspend all work on the Singapore defences and called an international conference on naval disarmament. As we have seen in the previous chapter, the London Naval Disarmament Conference resulted in further limitations on the size and armament of warships. All this meant a very welcome and considerable potential saving of government expenditure in those financially straitened times.

Despite the decision to suspend work on the defences of the naval base, some work did continue, and in 1931 two 6in BL guns on 15° mountings were installed at Gun Hill in the Changi district to cover the eastern entrance to the Strait of Johore. This proved not to be an ideal peacetime site as the guns were unable to fire on full charge through fear of damaging a number of nearby married quarters and the houses of Changi village.

In addition, the number of 3in 20cwt AA guns *in situ* had increased from two to eight. This was still only a third of the number that had been recommended for the defence of the island in 1925. Then the Singapore sub-committee had recommended a total of twenty-four guns in six groups of four, three groups for the Northern area, one for the Eastern and two for the Southern, an allocation that failed totally to take into account just

A 3in 20cwt AA gun manned by gunners of the Hong Kong & Singapore RA. The gun crew is carrying out practice firing at a site on the south coast of the island. (*Peter Stubbs*)

how many guns would be actually required to produce an effective barrage against air attack.

As we have seen, the 'Shanghai Incident' in 1932 was taken by the British government to be a clear warning of Japan's future intentions. The Chiefs of Staff pressed strongly for the resumption of work on the naval base and in October of that year put forward plans for the first stage of Singapore's re-armament. These were to include three 15in BL guns; six 9.2in Mark X guns on 35° mountings and ten 6in Mark VII guns, with a completion date for all set at 1936/7.

Although one mounting for one of the 15in guns had been completed by 1932, there was no question of mounting these guns within twelve months; and although the 9.2in counter-bombardment (CB) gun batteries could be installed within that period, they would not have permanent, adequate magazine accommodation. To compensate for the lack of heavy guns the War Office suggested that ten 9.2in BL guns on railway mountings could be made serviceable in nine months and railway spurs be constructed in

HMS *Terror* was an Erebus-class monitor built in 1915, and armed with two 15in BL guns. With a primary role of shore bombardment, the warship was stationed at Singapore until the construction of the two 15in shore batteries was complete. (*Author's collection*)

the same period. This suggestion was not taken up, and it was left to the Royal Navy in 1937 to offer the monitor HMS *Terror*, armed with two 15in BL guns. Moored off Pulau Ubin, the ship acted as a floating battery and stopgap armament until the land-based 15in guns were installed.

Chapter 9

The Approach of War: 1934–1941

The withdrawal of Japan from the League of Nations in 1933 was a further signal to the British government that work should recommence on the Singapore base. The Committee of Imperial Defence gave approval for an accelerated programme of artillery installation, which included the two 6in (152mm) guns and DELs for Pasir Laba on the west of the island, with a completion date of 1934/5. As part of the programme, initially as a temporary measure, four naval 6in guns were proposed, two for the defence of the west strait at Tanjong Karong and two for Tanjong Punggol on the north shore of the Island.[1] Initially, the plan was for these guns to be mounted on concrete platforms as used by the Royal Navy Mobile Base Defence Organisation, but subsequently it was decided that the mountings and emplacements should be Army pattern. Eventually, construction of these two batteries was cancelled.

With the General Staff still firmly of the view that any assault on Singapore would come from the south, and the decision having been taken that work should resume on arming the base, the approved armament was now:

3 x 15in (380mm) BL guns.
6 x 9.2in (233mm) BL guns on 35° mountings in two three-gun batteries.
6 x 6in BL guns on 15° mountings in three two-gun batteries.
2 x 6in BL guns on 45° mountings in one two-gun battery
24 x AA guns
10 x DELs

The estimated cost of this re-arming was estimated to be in the region of £1.5 million, and it was noted that the manufacture of mountings for two of the 15in BL guns would take four years, with a further year to instal them.

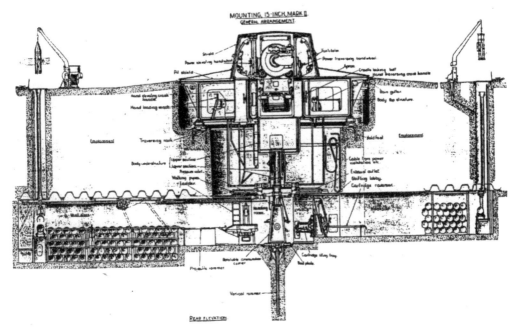

Cross-section drawing of a 15in BL gun on a Mark II (Spanish) mounting. (*John Roberts*)

In the counter-bombardment role, it had been planned that the three 15in guns would be mounted, two of them in a battery at Bee Hoe and one in a position on Blakang Mati. However, as a result of a survey of the latter it became clear that the position selected did not permit the gun to cover a certain area near the western entrance and was too open to observation. So it was decided that the third gun should be installed in a new position on the main island.

There was also a change in the types of mounting on which the three 15in guns were to be installed. The two types of available mounting were the Mark I or 'Singapore' with a traverse of 180°, and the Mark II or 'Spanish' with a greater traverse of 270°. The latter was so named as it was being manufactured for the Spanish government by Vickers Armstrong. The Mark I was the simpler of the two mountings, with a system of manual loading and magazines that were sited to the rear of the gun. The Mark II, on the other hand, was more sophisticated, resembling a naval turret and traversing on a huge roller ring, with automatic loading and magazines, engine room and

One of the 15in BL guns of Johore Battery in 1940. (*IWM K758*)

crew quarters. These were all underground, beneath a 15ft (4.6m) cover of concrete and earth, with flash-proof doors protecting the shell and cartridge stores. The cartridge and shell stores were echeloned, one on each flank of the gun position, with the power house in the rear linked by a 10yd (9.2m) passage.

Since range-finding at the extreme limit of 30,000yds (27,700m) was a major difficulty, the largest range-finder in the world was installed in Singapore. This Barr and Stroud FZ 100ft (30.75m) mechanism was originally developed in 1922 and mounted at Dover, before being transferred to Singapore. Trials of the range-finder found it to be accurate to 17yds at 31,000 yards (28,600m). A smaller 30ft (9.2m) range-finder was installed at the Changi Fire Control Centre.

The two three-gun 9.2in gun batteries were to be sited as follows: one on Pulau Tekong Besar to defend the eastern entrance to the Strait of Johore, and the other at Fort Connaught on Blakang Mati to guard Keppel Harbour.

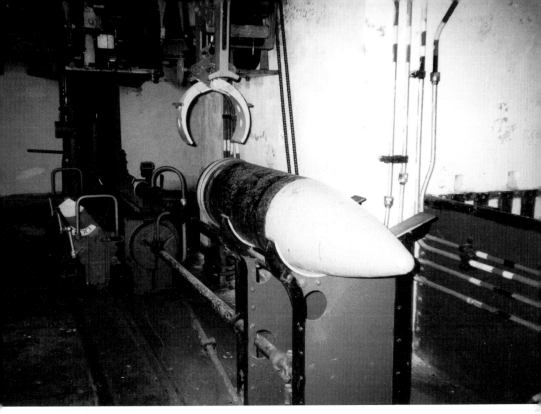

Ammunition-handling mechanism for the 15in BL gun on a Mark II (Spanish) mounting. This photograph shows the mechanism for one of the Vickers guns at La Mola on the island of Menorca, but the Singapore gun's mechanism was similar. (*Author's photograph*)

That on Pulau Tekong Besar would be a new battery on a virgin site, while at Fort Connaught the old guns would be removed and the fort rebuilt to take the new guns and mountings. To facilitate construction of the new batteries, a network of narrow-gauge railways was built to move the guns and mountings into position; these were subsequently used to move ammunition to the batteries from the main fortress magazine on Mount Faber.

Three of the 6in batteries on 15° mountings were already in place at Fort Siloso, Silingsing Battery and the new battery at Changi Point, and construction was starting on the new battery at Pasir Laba. Construction of the new battery on 45° mountings had been approved, and work was starting on the battery position close to the new 9.2in battery on Pulau Tekong Besar, thus providing the eastern channel with powerful defences against naval attack.

Construction of the two batteries on Pulau Tekong Besar was hampered by technical and medical problems. Their remote location on a roadless island meant that a light railway system had first to be built in order to

The largest in the world, the Barr & Stroud 100ft (30m) rangefinder was transferred in the 1930s from an experimental position at Dover to Singapore to support the 15in guns. The photograph shows it under test at the Barr & Stroud factory in Glasgow. (*Glasgow University*)

carry the building materials and then the guns and mountings to the battery sites. Then the civilian labour force contracted malaria, with some twenty labourers dying of the disease. Work stopped for a number of weeks while a massive anti-malarial campaign was waged, all standing water being sprayed with oil.

The new armament was to be formed into East and West Fire Commands, each manned by a heavy brigade (regiment) Royal Artillery. The East Fire Command was to comprise the batteries on Pulau Tekong Besar, Changi Point and Bee Hoe, while the West, also manned by a heavy brigade, would control the batteries on Blakang Mati and Silingsing Battery on Pulau Brani.

In 1932 the War Office had ordered the establishment of a new fortress observation system in Singapore, and two fortress fire control centres were set up, one at Changi and the other on Mount Faber. The fortress system was designed to cope with the increased ranges of which the guns on the new mountings were now capable. This system involved the use of a number of observation posts positioned from 4,000 to 10,000yds (3,692 to 9,230m) apart, sited to observe all the areas within range of the counter-bombardment guns. These observation posts, using depression position finders and range-finders, fed their bearings and ranges to the appropriate fortress fire control centre, where the fortress plotter equipment converted the ranges and bearings into map co-ordinates. The map co-ordinates were then sent by telephone, or later by Magslip (linked electric motors operating as transmitter and receiver), to the battery engaging the target, where they were converted into battery bearings and ranges.

The Battery Observation Post for Fort Connaught in 1938. Built on the top of Mount Serapong, it still remains, though heavily overgrown. (*TNA WO 203/6034*)

The approved number of anti-aircraft guns on the island had been increased from eight to twenty-four, in three batteries, two manned by men of the Royal Artillery and one by Indian gunners of the Hong Kong and Singapore Royal Artillery. The DELs in East Fire Command were to be the responsibility of a Fortress Company Royal Engineers, and those under the West Fire Command were manned by the Singapore Royal Engineers Straits Settlements Volunteer Force.

While the British Cabinet was contemplating the increasing threat of Japanese belligerence in the Far East since that country had recently renounced the Washington Treaty, a new danger was appearing much closer to home. In 1933 Adolf Hitler came to power, and in 1935 Germany repudiated the Versailles Treaty, which had ended the First World War, by introducing military conscription and re-arming in contravention of the treaty. Suddenly, Britain was faced with a potential new enemy, and in an attempt to mitigate the growing threat of another naval race with Germany, negotiated the Anglo-German Naval Treaty in June 1935. This treaty permitted Germany to increase the size of its small navy, but limited it to

A 3.7in HAA gun manned by gunners of the Hong Kong & Singapore RA. (*IWM K505*)

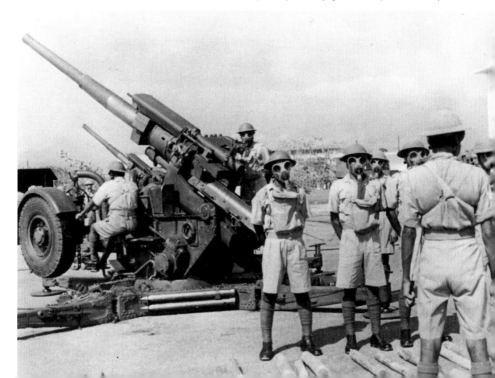

35 per cent of the Royal Navy's tonnage. With the possibility of Britain facing a renewed German naval threat, albeit from a force one a third the size of the Royal Navy, it now seemed less likely that a major fleet could be released from home waters to reinforce Singapore.

In 1932 the British government had formally abandoned the 'Ten Year Rule', stating, however, that the abandonment of the rule should not be taken as justifying any increased expenditure on the armed forces. However, by 1934 it was clear to the government that there was now an urgent need to make good the deficiencies in the equipment of the armed forces, and a limited programme of re-armament was authorized, made even more urgent by the Italian invasion of Abyssinia in 1935, which only served to emphasize the world's uncertain political state.

The Barron Report

In February 1935 Major General F. W. Barron, Inspector of Fixed Defences at the War Office, reached Singapore on an inspection visit of all fixed defences in the Far East. On arrival he indicated that the objects of his visit were to determine whether the siting of Singapore's fixed defences was effective in view of their role, and to report on whether additional defences should be included in the second stage of the arming of the base.

General Barron reviewed the locations of all the existing and proposed batteries and presented his views to the General Officer Commanding Malaya Command, Major General E. O. Lewin, and his staff. In reviewing the counter-bombardment batteries General Barron noted that a single 15in BL Mark I gun at Buona Vista Battery, the new site on the mainland, was approved for the first stage, with two Mark II guns to be added in the second stage. General Barron rejected this proposal, since in his view a single 15in gun was of little or no value. Instead, he proposed that this gun should be mounted at Bee Hoe, making that a three-gun battery, and suggested that in its place at Buona Vista a three-gun 9.2in battery should be installed.[2]

On the whole, the general agreed with the position of existing and proposed 6in batteries, but he took note of the War Office's concerns regarding the existing defences of Keppel Harbour. As early as 1932, the Committee of Imperial Defence had expressed doubts regarding these defences, particularly considering that the floating dock was anchored there and major fuel storage facilities were sited on the harbour shore. General Barron recommended, therefore, that the existing defences be reinforced by the addition of three 6in close defence batteries, each of two guns. One battery was to be sited in the old Fort Pasir Panjang; the second on Blakang Mati, with one gun in the old 9.2in battery emplacement on Serapong Spur and the other in a new emplacement nearby; and the third battery at Beting Kusah, south-east of Changi village on the main island.

In 1935 authority was received for the construction of these, and the new battery on the site of the old Fort Pasir Panjang, now named Labrador Battery, was given the role of supporting the 6in QF guns at Fort Siloso by giving depth to the defence of Keppel Harbour. Although the original suggestion was that the guns of the new battery should be mounted in the quick-firing gun emplacements of the old fort, the eventual decision was that the old emplacement for the 9.2in BL Mark IV No 1 gun should be

This 1940 propaganda photograph shows a 6in Mk VII BL gun probably at Labrador Battery. The gun is fitted with a locally manufactured anti-splinter shield and manned by gunners of the HKSRA. (*IWM K704*)

demolished and two emplacements for the 6in BL Mark VII guns built in its place. The old magazine was adapted for the new guns, and the existing casemates were adapted to contain an engine room and oil store. Two DELs and a position-finding cell were built nearby.

The battery at Changi Point was unusual in being sited a mere 18ft (5.5m) above sea level, and this necessitated the Battery Observation Post being mounted on a metal-framed tower 78ft (23.75m) high, similar to the battery observation tower of Cornwallis battery at Georgetown on Penang Island.

General Lewin, himself a gunner by profession, did not agree with the proposal to move the Buona Vista gun to Bee Hoe, recommending instead that a second 15in gun should be added to the battery as part of the first stage, rather than waiting for the yet to be commenced second stage.

It was now that fate, in the person of the Sultan of Johore, stepped in to take a hand. The Sultan, a fervent anglophile with a Scottish wife, offered the British government the huge sum of £500,000 as a gift to celebrate the silver jubilee of King George V, and the Committee of Imperial Defence decided that £400,000 of this money should be allocated to completing the two 15in gun batteries. The decision was taken to follow General Barron's proposal to add the gun on the Mark I (Singapore) mounting to the two guns on Mark II (Spanish) mountings to be installed at Bee Hoe, and the position was re-named Johore Battery in honour of the Sultan. At Buona Vista the battery was to comprise two guns on Mark II (Spanish) mountings, making a total of five 15in BL guns.

To provide for the re-supply of ammunition in the Changi area a metre-gauge railway was built linking the pier at Fairy Point to the main magazine at Changi Hill and the three guns of Johore Battery. This railway was subsequently to prove vulnerable to air attack during the Japanese invasion in 1942.

Major General Lewin handed over his command to Major General William Dobbie in November 1935. Having been commissioned into the Royal Engineers, Dobbie took a particular interest in the defences of Singapore and firmly believed that in order to defend the island it would be necessary to defend Malaya itself. Unlike his predecessors, Dobbie was not convinced that the country north of Singapore was impassable to an enemy advance. He therefore turned his attention to adding more fixed defences, and submitted a plan to the War Office for the construction of works in southern Johore, but nothing came of it.

However, General Dobbie was instrumental in authorizing the construction of a number of pillboxes along what became known as the Jitra Line in northern Malaya, as well as at Kota Tinggi and Kota Bahru on the mainland north of Singapore. He was also responsible for the construction of the one close defence battery to be built on the mainland. Concerned about the defence of the main channel leading to the naval base, and at the fact that Calder Passage was now known to be navigable, he believed that a battery was required at Pengerang. This would strengthen the defences of the main channel and, at the same time, provide direct defence of the Calder Passage.

Although there were some doubts about the remote location of such a battery and the requirement for infantry to defend it, approval was given for the construction of a battery of two 6in BL guns on 15° mountings. Construction began in 1937 and the battery was completed in 1939. It was subsequently provided with the overhead concrete splinter cover provided for other batteries, but did not receive the anti-splinter shields as at Labrador Battery, simply retaining the old, low armoured shields. The reason for this may have been because it was planned to replace the Mark VII guns with more modern Mark XXIV pieces from the May/June production in 1942.[3]

In 1933 the decision was taken to complete the base's defences in three and a half years. The total cost came to a total of £1,639,000, which was to be spread over four years as follows:

1933/4	£214,000
1934/5	£700,000
1935/6	£475,000
1936/7	£250,000[4]

By 1936 the fixed defences were finally taking shape as follows:

a. Faber (West) Fire Command
Buona Vista Battery. 2 x 15in Mark I BL guns on Mark II mountings (45°).

Fort Connaught. 3 x 9.2in Mark X BL guns on Mark VII mountings (35°).

Labrador Battery. 2 x 6in Mark VII BL guns on Central Pivot mountings Mark II (15°).

Silingsing Battery. 2 x 6in Mark VII BL guns on Central Pivot mountings Mark II (15°).

Fort Siloso. 2 x 6in Mark VII BL guns on Central Pivot mountings Mark II (15°).

Pasir Laba. 2 x 6in Mark VII BL guns on Central Pivot mountings Mark II (15°).

Serapong Spur Battery. 2 x 6in Mark VII BL guns on Central Pivot mountings Mark II (15°).

b. Changi (East) Fire Command
Johore Battery. 2 x 15in Mark I BL guns on Mark II mountings (45°).

1 x 15in Mark I BL gun on Mark I mounting (55°).

Tekong Besar Battery. 3 x 9.2in Mark X BL guns on Mark VII mountings (35°).

Changi Battery. 2 x 6in Mark VII BL guns on Central Pivot Mark II mountings (15°).

Beting Kusah Battery. 2 x 6in Mark VII BL guns on Central Pivot Mark II mountings (15°).

Pengerang Battery. 2 x 6in Mark VII BL guns on Central Pivot Mark II mountings (15°).

Sphinx Battery (Pulau Tekong). 2 x 6in Mark XXIV BL guns on Mark V mountings (45°).[5]

As a result of the re-arming of Fort Connaught, the 9.2in gun batteries on Mount Serapong, Serapong Spur and Mount Imbeah were decommissioned and their guns removed, though the Mount Imbeah battery remained in use as the reserve magazine for Blakang Mati.

At the same time as the armament was finally approved for the defence of Keppel Harbour and the naval base, firm decisions were also made regarding the siting of the DELs. In addition to the previously existing four lights at Fort Siloso and Silingsing Battery, a further twelve lights, all concentrated beam (fighting) lights, were approved. These were to be sited in pairs at Labrador Battery, Changi Spit, Beting Kusah Battery, Sphinx Battery on Pulau Tekong Besar and Batu Kusah; also on Pulau Tekong Besar and at Pengerang on the Johore mainland.[6]

In 1937 instructions were given that all 6in guns were to have all-round traverse in their emplacements, and in 1938 HMS *Terror*, a monitor armed with two 15in guns, arrived in Singapore. This warship was to act as a floating battery until the two 15in batteries were completed and operational. All these defences were now considered essential: not only was the political situation in Europe increasingly threatening, but in 1938 the Admiralty announced that the period before a fleet could be expected to reach Singapore had now been extended to ninety days rather than the forty-two as previously envisaged.

The Buona Vista Battery was completed in 1939 but, as with the Changi close defence battery, there were restrictions on practice firing. The battery was three miles (4.8km) from the sea, and shells from the guns passed over the land of a rich Chinese rubber concern. The owners protested about the trial firing, claiming one million Singapore dollars for 'injurious affection' [*sic*]. To avoid a lengthy and possibly expensive legal suit, the trial firing was carried out with a limited arc of 3°, which resulted in the shells being fired over government land. The gun crews later practised using the guns of Johore Battery.[7]

The anti-motor torpedo boat defences

As we have seen, by 1935 the whole concept of an attack by coastal motor boats, or motor torpedo boats as they were now termed, had been re-assessed. On 21 November 1935 the Lords of the Admiralty wrote to the Chiefs of Staff Committee reviewing the Admiralty position on the likelihood of such an attack, in view of the development of fast commercial-type motor boats which could be quickly purchased by an enemy. In the opinion of their Lordships, these boats could be transported to Singapore in cruisers or merchantmen, and an attack on Keppel Harbour, or even on the naval anchorage in the

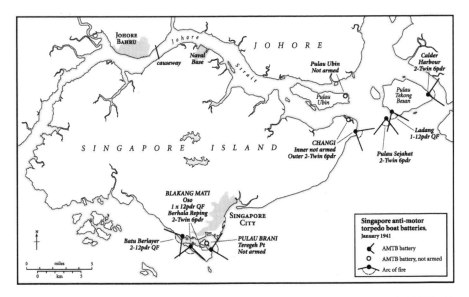

Map of the anti-motor torpedo Boat defences installed in Singapore in the period 1938–41. (*Martin Brown*)

Strait of Johore, was now considered a possibility to be taken more seriously.[8] Seven years earlier, the Gillman Commission had selected sites for batteries of Twin 6pdr QF equipments, and General Barron had recommended that two anti-coastal motor boat (AMTB) guns be installed at Pasir Panjang (Batu Berlayer) in the old 12pdr QF gun emplacements, together with four DELs. The Committee of Imperial Defence approved the mounting of Twin 6pdr QF equipments at Pasir Panjang, while also approving a further two such equipments, three DELs and an anti-motor torpedo boat boom for the defence of the eastern entrance to Keppel Harbour.

In December 1936 the Joint Oversea and Home Defence sub-committee of the Committee of Imperial Defence recommended that a total of nineteen Twin 6pdr equipments should be provided for the defence of the naval anchorage and dockyard and Keppel Harbour, at a cost of £592,000. The Committee of Imperial Defence gave its formal approval to this proposal on 3 March 1937. The deployment of these guns was to be as follows:

Outer defences of Main Harbour

i.	West of Tekong Besar	
	Changi Spit	2 equipments
	Pulau Sejahat	2 equipments
ii.	West coast of Tekong Besar	1 equipment
iii.	East of Tekong Besar	2 equipments

Inner defences of Main Harbour

i.	South of Pulau Ubin	
	Changi PS	2 equipments
ii.	North of Pulau Ubin	
	On Pulau Ubin	2 equipments

Defences of Keppel Harbour

i.	East Entrance	
	Berhala Reping	2 equipments
	Tanjong Tereh	1 equipment
ii.	West Entrance	
	Siloso	1 equipment
	Pulau Hantu	1 equipment
	BatuBerlayer	2 equipments

One reserve equipment was to be provided, and the provision of ammunition was to be 2,000 rounds plus a reserve of 1,000 per equipment.

To support these new guns it was planned that a total of thirty-three DELs should be installed, with twenty to cover the approaches to the Main Harbour and thirteen for Keppel Harbour.[9] These lights were of two types, fixed and fighting. The fixed beam DELs were positioned in brick or concrete positions, each with a number of narrow vertical slits which permitted areas of water to be illuminated at angles of 16°, 30° or 45°. The fighting lights had moveable beams which permitted the light to follow a target, in the same manner as anti-aircraft searchlights.

On 4 November 1937 the Committee gave final approval for the anti-motor torpedo boat defences at the eastern entrance to the Strait of Johore. Two Twin 6pdr QF batteries were to be installed on Pulau Tekong Besar, with

The photograph, taken in 1946, shows the fire control tower of one of the two Twin 6pdr QF equipments at Calder Harbour Battery. (*TNA WO203/6034*)

similar batteries at Calder Harbour, and one equipment at Ladang. Work commenced on the structures of the batteries some time after 1 November 1938 and was completed some nine months later, two months before the outbreak of war with Germany on 3 September 1939. However, in 1938 the precise number of guns and lights for the western entrance to Keppel Harbour was still under discussion with the local authorities in Singapore.

The situation regarding the arming of these anti-motor torpedo boat batteries was to become something of a game of musical chairs. Although the gun positions and director towers were completed by 1940, none of the Twin 6pdr equipments had been delivered because of the situation in Europe. In August 1940 the General Officer Commanding Malaya Command, Major General Leslie Bond, received notification from the War Office that due to what was termed 'the necessary diversion to Home requirements' of the Twin 6pdr equipments, it was impossible to forecast when such guns would become available for Singapore.

Four 12pdr QF guns were dispatched from Britain in the late summer of 1940 and these were to be installed in some of the newly constructed Twin 6pdr emplacements. General Bond advised the War Office that the sites selected for the guns were Ladang, Berhala Reping (two guns) and Labrador Battery, but the War Office revised the selection of these sites, ordering the guns for Berhala Reping to be moved to Changi. In fact, it would appear that the two 12pdr guns remained at Berhala Reping until March 1941, when two Twin 6pdr QF equipments arrived in Singapore and were mounted there. The two 12pdr QF guns were then, finally, mounted, one at Labrador Battery and the other at Fort Siloso. Two of the anti-motor torpedo boat batteries constructed for the defence of the eastern entrance to the Strait of Johore, Pulau Ubin and Changi Inner, were never armed. The scale of ammunition for the four 12pdr QF guns was officially 1,000 rounds per gun, but the first two guns were delivered with only 500 rounds apiece, and the second two with only 250.[10]

To summarize, therefore, by early 1942 the anti-motor torpedo boat batteries and their armament were as follows:

Changi Fire Command

Changi Outer (Palm)	2 x Twin 6pdr QF equipments
Changi Inner (School)	never armed
Calder Harbour	2 x Twin 6pdr QF equipments
Ladang	1 x 12pdr QF gun
Pulau Sejahat (Tekong)	2 x Twin 6pdr QF equipments
Pulau Ubin	never armed

Faber Fire Command

Batu Berlayer	2 x Twin 6pdr QF equipments
Pulau Hantu	1 x 18pdr QF field gun
Oso (Fort Siloso)	1 x 12pdr QF gun
Berhala Reping	2 x Twin 6pdr QF equipments
Tanjong Tereh (Pulau Brani)	never armed

Additional defences were provided in the form of anti-motor torpedo boat booms, an anti-submarine indicator loop and controlled minefields. These were laid to close the eastern entrance to the Johore Strait between Changi Point and Pulau Tekong Besar, across the entrance to Calder Harbour and between Changi and Pulau Ubin and Pulau Ubin and the Johore mainland. Both entrances to Keppel Harbour were similarly protected. In January 1941 HMS *Redstart*, a coastal mine- and net-layer, later to be lost when the Japanese invaded Hong Kong, was dispatched from Hong Kong to Singapore and spent several months laying controlled minefields between Changi and Pulau Tekong Besar and across the eastern entrance to Keppel Harbour.

The anti-aircraft defences

By 1938 work was well under way to construct the new defences: counter-bombardment, close defence and anti-motor torpedo boat. Only the anti-aircraft defence of the island still lagged behind. In 1927 there were only two heavy anti-aircraft guns in the colony, both of which were 3in (76mm) 20cwt guns dating from the First World War. However, at the time this model was the only effective anti-aircraft weapon available to the Army, since production of the famous 3.7in (94mm) HAA gun did not start until ten years later.

In 1927 the Committee of Imperial Defence agreed that Singapore should have a total of twenty-four anti-aircraft guns, with a further fourteen being added to the two currently *in situ* between 1927 and 1930. A further eight guns were to be provided in the period 1931–7.[11]

By 1937 the 3in 20cwt AA gun was being superseded by the 4.5in (115mm) HAA gun and the new 3.7in HAA gun, both on static mountings for the defence of urban areas and the latter in a trailer-mounted version for use with the field force. The new 3.7in HAA guns were much more powerful weapons than the older 3in AA piece and were used in conjunction with predictors made by Vickers and Sperry, Barr and Stroud height-finders, sound locators and searchlights. In December 1938 approval was given for the construction of concrete platforms for four 4.5in HAA guns and four 3in AA guns for practice purposes. As a temporary measure in June 1938, twenty-four 3in Naval AA guns were dispatched from Colombo on loan, pending provision of more modern equipment. However, these guns were not provided with fire control equipment and required permanent emplacements; and, to cap it all, there were insufficient gunners to man them!

In 1936 the approved air defence for Singapore was to consist of a total of seventy-two guns: twenty-four 3.7in HAA guns and forty-eight 4.5in HAA guns, together with 114 anti-aircraft searchlights. In fact, the 4.5in HAA guns were required for the air defence of Great Britain, and only two of these were actually delivered, in September 1939, so 3.7in HAA guns, both static and mobile, were substituted. When war came to Singapore in February 1941 there were forty-one of these guns, twenty-seven on static mountings and fourteen mobile, to defend the Island, together with twenty of the older 3in 20cwt AA guns. In addition, there were the two heavier 4.5in HAA guns.[12]

For point defence against low-flying aircraft the British Army used the Bofors 40mm LAA gun. In 1937 the War Office had approved sixteen of these guns for the defence of the naval base, allocated as follows:

Floating Dock	2
Graving Dock	2
Generating Station	3
Oil Fuel Depot	9[13]

The very large number allocated to the defence of the oil fuel depot was due to its immense size. At a subsequent meeting of the Joint Oversea and Home Defence Committee, later that year, the provision of a further six guns was approved, two for the defence of the Woodland fuel depot near the naval base, and four for defence of the aircraft storage depot at Seletar. By December 1941 another twelve guns had been added, bringing the total to thirty-four altogether. Additional HAA and LAA guns may have arrived on the Island with the retreating field force, but it is uncertain how many, because there appears to be no official record of them.

The garrison anti-aircraft guns were deployed to provide defence against air attack for the naval base, the fuel depots and the airfields at Seletar, Tengah, Sembawang and Kalang. The two 4.5in HAA guns were deployed at Nee Soon East in the centre of the island. The guns were manned by both British and Indian soldiers of the Royal Artillery, the Hong Kong and

Singapore Royal Artillery and the Indian Artillery, and firing practices were held at Beting Kusah on the coast, where the guns fired from permanent concrete platforms on the foreshore.

Anti-aircraft searchlight cover was provided by 5th Searchlight Regiment RA, which was formed on 15 May 1941, comprising four searchlight batteries, 13th,14th, 315th and 316th SL Batteries RA. Four lights manned by 14th Battery illuminated the Johore causeway, while members of 316th Battery were trained to man eight Bofors LAA guns.[14]

HMS *Redstart*, a coastal minelayer of 500 tons built in 1938. This vessel laid the observation minefields in Singapore, but was later sunk in December 1941 in Hong Kong. (*Author's collection*)

Chapter 10

The Battle for Singapore

Gunners and guns

By late 1941 the troops manning the fixed defences of Singapore were a mixture of men from the Royal Artillery and the Hong Kong and Singapore Royal Artillery. The latter was a unit of the British Army directly descended from the company of artillery lascars formed in Singapore in 1891. Subsequently, a similar company, part of the garrison of Hong Kong, joined the Singapore company to form the Singapore and Hong Kong Battalion, Royal Garrison Artillery, one company of which was stationed in Singapore. Finally, in 1924 it was renamed the Hong Kong and Singapore Royal Artillery (HKSRA).

The garrison of the fixed defences comprised three regiments: the 7th Coast Regiment RA, with the 11th and 31st Coast Batteries RA and the 5th and 7th Batteries HKSRA; the 9th Coast Regiment RA, with 7th, 22nd and 32nd Coast Batteries RA; and the 16th Defence Regiment RA, less one battery, which had the role of manning the beach defences of Singapore Island with the 966th Battery RA, 967th and 968th Batteries HKSRA under command. The 16th Defence Regiment RA had been formed in 1939, originally as 10th Mobile Coast Regiment RA, being renamed in 1941. It was armed with First World War 18pdr QF field guns and two 3pdr QF guns of even older vintage, one of which was mounted on the hulk *Loudon* to defend the Keppel Harbour boom, the other on the Detached Mole.

The batteries of Faber Fire Command were manned by men of the 7th Coast Regiment RA, commanded by Lieutenant Colonel H. D. St G. Cardew, while the 9th Coast Regiment RA, commanded by Lieutenant Colonel C. P. Heath, manned the guns of Changi Fire Command. The batteries of the two Fire Commands were manned by the following units:

Faber Fire Command
11th Coast Battery RA
Fort Connaught (3 x 9.2in (233mm) CB guns)
Serapong Battery (2 x 6in (152mm) CD guns)
Berhala Reping AMTB Battery (2 x twin 6pdr QF equipments)
Pulau Hantu AMTB Battery (1 x 18pdr QF field gun)
31st Coast Battery RA
Buona Vista Battery (2 x 15in (380mm) CB guns)
Batu Berlayer AMTB Battery (2 x 12pdr QF gun)
5th Battery HKSRA
Silingsing Battery (2 x 6in CD guns)
Oso (Siloso Point) AMTB Battery (1 x 12pdr QF gun)
7th Battery HKSRA
Labrador Battery (2 x 6in CD guns)
Pasir Laba Battery (2 x 6in CD guns)

Changi Fire Command
7th Coast Battery RA
Johore Battery (3 x 15in CB guns)
Beting Kusah Battery (2 x 6in CD guns)
22nd Coast Battery RA
Tekong Besar Battery (3 x 9.2in CB guns)
Sphinx Battery (2 x 6in CB guns)
Ladang AMTB Battery (1 x 12pdr QF gun)
Pulau Sejahat AMTB Battery (2 x twin 6pdr QF equipments)
32nd Coast Battery RA
Pengerang Battery (2 x 6in CD guns)
Changi Battery (2 x 6in CD guns)
Tanjong Johore Battery, Pengerang (2 x 18pdr QF field guns)
Calder Harbour AMTB Battery (2 x twin 6pdr QF equipments)

The AMTB batteries at Batu Berlayer, Oso (Fort Siloso) and Ladang were temporarily equipped with old 12pdr QF guns in lieu of the planned Twin 6pdr equipments, which were not due to arrive in Singapore until July and August 1942.

The CASLs of Fort Siloso provided illumination for both the 6in close defence guns of Fort Siloso and the Oso and Batu Berlayer anti-motor torpedo boat batteries. (*Author's photograph*)

By the end of 1941 most of the 6in close defence batteries had been provided with overhead concrete protection and improved shields. The exceptions were the Pasir Laba Battery which, although provided with concrete splinter protection, had only the standard semi-circular armoured shields, and Silingsing Battery on Pulau Brani that had light, splinter-proof shields, which provided some protection for the guns and the gun-layers. The uncovered guns of Changi Battery retained their 360° traverse and were fitted with anti-splinter shields over the top of the breech. However, those batteries provided with concrete overhead cover now had the traverse of their guns considerably limited by the new overhead protection.

The whole concept of the siting of the Singapore fixed defences was to defend the Island and the naval base from attack by sea. Despite the modern myth that the guns of Singapore pointed the wrong way, most of the guns originally had sufficient traverse to enable fire to be brought down on parts of the Johore mainland. However, when the base was first planned it was firmly believed by the military authorities that an attack from the north was most unlikely due to the nature of the country, which was considered impassable to major troop movements.

Of all the Army commanders in Malaya prior to the Second World War only General Dobbie fully appreciated that Singapore and the naval base were vulnerable to attack from the north. On his orders a start had been made on the construction of field fortifications at Jitra in northern Malaya and at Kota Tinggi in Johore to defend the northern approach to Singapore. However, the accepted military view at that time was that since Malaya was flanked by French Indo-China and neutral Siam (Thailand), any attack on Singapore by Japan must, necessarily, come from the sea. The decision was taken, therefore, to protect the seaward side of the island and, with the exception of the 15in Mark I gun at Johore Battery, all the guns of the fixed defences initially had a traverse of at least 270°. However, only the two 15in pieces of Johore Battery on Mark II mountings were capable of firing on Johore Bahru and the Causeway, as the limited traverse of the gun on the Mark I mounting (180°) prevented it from doing so. In addition, the guns of Buona Vista Battery were unable to traverse as they were fitted with gun-stops which limited their movement.

Two theories for the fitting of these gun-stops have been advanced. One is that the 'Magslip' fire control cabling, which allowed the gun to be fired remotely, was too short; the other is that the gun-stops were necessary to protect the 'walking' cables. In his book *Did Singapore Have To Fall?* the author, Kevin Blackburn, says that as the 'walking' cables carried the hydraulic power to the gun mounting, assisting the traverse, elevation and loading of the gun, so disconnecting these cables to improve the traverse would mean the gun would have to be loaded and trained manually without any power assistance. This would dramatically slow the rate of fire.[1]

As we have seen, many of the guns had the ability to engage targets on the Johore mainland, only to have this capability restricted by overhead concrete cover. Added to this restriction on their effectiveness to engage land targets was the problem of ammunition. When coastal artillery engaged warships the requirement was to penetrate the ship's armour, and high-explosive and shrapnel shells had little effect on such targets. However, armour-piercing shells were of little use against enemy personnel and artillery.

Brigadier A. D. Curtis, commanding the Malayan fixed defences, stated in the War Diary for Singapore's coastal defences compiled after the battle for the Island that there were only fifty high-explosive shells available for each 6in gun, twenty-five of these rounds for each 9.2in, and none at all for the 15in guns.[2] There is some contradiction here, as the same source gives a

One of the Singapore 15in BL guns carrying out a practice firing. (*IWM K755*)

figure of thirty high-explosive shells for each 9.2in gun, and also mentions that a single 15in high-explosive shell was obtained from the ammunition depot in the naval base. One can only wonder how that single shell came to be stored in the depot and hope that, when fired by a gun of Johore Battery, it succeeded in finding a worthwhile target.

Additional high-explosive ammunition had been requested on 28 January 1942, and the War Office had authorized the dispatch of a hundred 9.2in shells from Ceylon and a further 350 from the United Kingdom, while the Admiralty authorized the dispatch of 250 shells for the 15in guns from the Mediterranean. Sadly, none would arrive before the surrender of the base.[3]

In January 1942 Brigadier Curtis gave orders that likely land targets in Johore opposite the north and west coasts of Singapore and north and east of Pengerang were to be registered. Nevertheless, the selection of such targets was limited by inadequate range or insufficient arcs of fire. In addition, it was felt by Brigadier Curtis and the officer commanding Buona Vista Battery that, as there was still the danger of an attack from the sea, the fire control cabling, which limited the all-round traverse of the guns, should be retained to enable the battery to counter such an attack. The battery was, therefore, unable to engage any targets to the north of its position.

As we shall see later in this chapter, some of the guns of the fixed defences did, in fact, engage Japanese targets both on the mainland, and on Singapore Island itself. Unfortunately, fewer than half the guns were able to engage these targets, and the very limited amount of high-explosive ammunition available reduced their effectiveness. However, CO 9 Coast Regiment RA established OPs on the north coast of Pulau Tekong Besar, and at Kitchener Barracks, Changi and Loyang, to control fire across the Johore Strait.

The beach defences

Just as the guns were sited to defend against an attack from the sea, so the bulk of the beach defences were constructed along the south-western, southern and south-eastern shores of Singapore Island. The permanent defences comprised concrete firing platforms for 18pdr QF field guns and pillboxes for medium and light machine guns, all manned by personnel of 16th Defence Regiment RA and the 1st Battalion the Manchester Regiment, a machine-gun battalion.

Prior to the Japanese invasion of Malaya more than sixty pillboxes of two main types were built to defend Singapore, running in a line from Pasir Laba on the west coast through Singapore Town to Changi village. Other pillboxes were built on Blakang Mati and Pulau Brani, and to defend Pengerang Battery on the Johore mainland. The designs of the two types of pillbox to be found in Malaya and Singapore appear to have been unique to the Far East. Similar pillboxes are to be found in Hong Kong and they differ markedly from those in the United Kingdom that were designed by the Fortifications and Works Branch of the War Office. The former have been described as 'Singapore and Kota Tinggi Type', and were designed by the Engineer Branch at HQ Malaya Command. They were constructed in the period 1938–41, and in a cable to the War Office in 1938 General Dobbie reported: 'Have standardized very satisfactorily concrete emplacements each for one Lyon light and two Bren guns or machine guns. Thirty-eight now in process of construction from existing funds on WD and Crown Lands together with effective wire obstacles. Thirty-eight more planned.'[4]

The two designs of pillbox can best be described as 'Type 1' and 'Type 2', with the Type 1 being square in shape, with approximate dimensions of 15ft (4.6m) wide by 15ft (4.6m) deep by 12ft (3.6m) high, and built of reinforced concrete. This design was notable in having a commander's observation cupola on top and two embrasures for machine-guns, both in the side facing the most likely direction of attack. This meant that these pillboxes were vulnerable to attack from the rear and the sides.

The Type 2 was a more sophisticated design altogether, comprising a central observation post, or sometimes a beach searchlight position, flanked by two low-level positions for machine-guns. The Type 2 was also built of reinforced concrete but, like Type 1, was vulnerable to attack from the rear and sides.

A Singapore Type 1 pillbox seen today at the junction of Science Park Road and Pasir Panjang Road in Singapore. These pillboxes were notable for having a commander's observation cupola, and only two firing embrasures facing forward. (*Author's photograph*)

One of the beach defence pillboxes built on the south coast of the island. This pillbox is on the beach at Labrador Park, and the machine gun embrasures on each side of the pillbox are currently buried in the sand. (*Author's photograph*)

The 16th Defence Regiment RA was armed with a total of twenty-four 18pdr QF field guns and twelve 2pdr anti-tank guns, the latter manned by the Royal Artillery battery. In addition, there were six 18pdr QF field guns manned by the Straits Settlements Volunteer Force battery and two sections of similar guns manned by HKSRA personnel. These men were from units in Hong Kong who were retained in Singapore on their way back to Hong Kong from leave in India. The southern beach defence areas were surveyed for a total of twenty-four positions, each for two 18pdr field guns and a beach searchlight, and numbered BD1 to BD24. BD1 was located 500yds (462m) from Pasir Laba Battery in the west, and BD24 was located to the west of Pengerang Battery

Each position for an 18pdr QF field gun was provided with a Hogg and Paul platform, originally developed at the end of the First World War in order to provide the gun with a limited traverse. The platform was actually a simple device comprising a spare spoked gun wheel laid horizontally on

An 18pdr QF field gun on a Paul & Hogg platform. A similar gun and mounting was in place on Pulau Hantu. The field gun wheel on which the gun pivoted can be seen beneath the gun. (*Author's collection*)

a square wooden base, itself laid on a concrete platform or a platform of wooden planks. The gun was then mounted on the platform.

On the northern shores of the island the state of the beach defences was another matter altogether. Very little had been done to put potential landing sites into any manner of defence, partly because of the generally unsuitable terrain, largely covered with mangrove, and partly because of the policy of the General Officer Commanding, Lieutenant General Percival.

In June 1941 Brigadier Ivan Simpson was sent to Singapore to take up the post of Chief Engineer Malaya Command with, according to Brigadier Simpson, specific verbal instructions 'to install the most modern types of defences throughout Malaya, including Singapore Island, and to bring all existing defences up-to-date, specifically against possible beach landings and against tank and air attack'.[5]

It would seem, however, that Brigadier Simpson's proposals were not accepted by General Percival, who stated firmly to the Brigadier his belief that 'Defences are bad for morale – for both troops and civilians.'[6] The Commander Singapore Fortress, Major General Keith Simmons, was also opposed to defence works on the landward side of the island for the same reason. Despite this rejection of anti-invasion defences on the north shore, defence stores, including barbed wire, pickets and tubular scaffolding for beach obstruction, were dumped at locations on the north shore on the orders of the Deputy Chief Engineer, but no attempt was made to construct pillboxes or anti-tank obstacles. So it was not until 23 January 1942 that General Percival, possibly as a result of prompting by General Wavell, Commander of the American-British-Dutch-Australian Command in Java, ordered defences to be prepared on the north shore! Sadly, this was far too little and much too late, and the back door to Singapore remained wide open!

The battle

War came to Malaya and Singapore on 8 December 1941, when Japanese troops landed at Singora and Patani in Siam (Thailand), on the northern border with the Federated Malay States. Advancing swiftly southwards, the Japanese brushed aside the British troops defending the half-completed

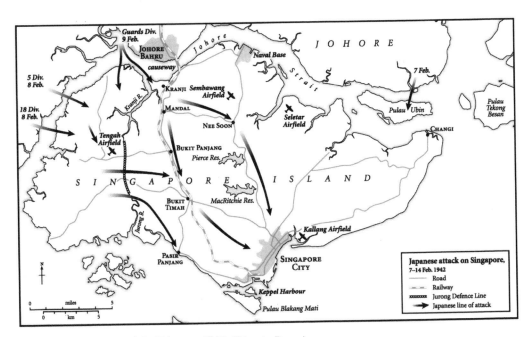

The Japanese attack in February 1942. (*Martin Brown*)

Jitra Line and pushed on down the west coast of Malaya. A further landing by Japanese troops at Kota Bahru on the east coast and the continuing advance by the Japanese on the west forced the British defenders to abandon the airfields at Alor Star and Butterworth. With the loss of these airfields, together with the sinking of the ships of the Royal Navy's Force Z, HMS *Prince of Wales* and HMS *Repulse,* the Japanese gained complete control of the air and sea.

Moving steadily southwards and driving the British forces before them, the Japanese divisions, spearheaded by tanks, advanced on Singapore. No anti-tank defences had been constructed to delay the Japanese armoured thrust along the few existing roads, and despite a short-lived stand at Gemas on the so-called 'Johore Line' the British were unable to repulse the invaders. Threatened by a further enemy advance along the west coast road, the British, Australian and Indian troops were forced to fall back on 'Fortress Singapore'.

The problem facing General Percival was how best to defend the Island. General Wavell had informed Percival that he expected Singapore to withstand a siege of up to two months but, in the end, the garrison held out for only two weeks. Percival's belief was that, in view of the Japanese command of the sea and air, he had to deploy his forces in such a way as to prevent an enemy landing anywhere on the Island, and so needed to defend the complete 72 miles (120 km) of coastline.

Percival divided Singapore into three defensive areas, Northern, Western, and Southern. The Southern Area comprised the coast east of the Causeway to Changi Point, including the island of Pulau Ubin; the Western Area comprised the coast westwards from the Causeway to the Jurong River in the south-west; and the Southern Area comprised the coast from the Jurong River to Changi, including the city of Singapore itself, Pulau Tekong Besar and the southern islands.

The Japanese commander, General Yamashita, planned to attack the Island by landing the bulk of his forces west of the Causeway, but obvious troop concentrations were assembled on the Johore mainland opposite Pulau Ubin. This apparent build-up was a feint by the Japanese, and Percival, lacking effective air reconnaissance and other intelligence, was duly deceived.

General Wavell believed, correctly, that the Japanese attack would come from the north-west and he advised Percival to deploy the newly-arrived 18th British Division in that area. General Percival, however, deployed his two Australian brigades and one Indian brigade in the Western Area, while in the Northern Area he deployed III Indian Corps, consisting of the three brigades of the 18th British Division and two under-strength brigades of the 11th Indian Division. In addition, the bulk of the field artillery was allocated to the Northern Area. The Southern Area was held by the Fortress troops of the fixed defences, two Malay infantry brigades and the Straits Settlements Volunteer Force. Two Indian brigades were retained as the Command Reserve.

In fact, war came first to the fixed defences on 6 January, when Blakang Mati was heavily bombed and there was damage to the 9.2in reserve gun at Fort Connaught and to a 6in gun and mounting at Serapong Spur battery. It was unfortunate that the vast majority of the coastal batteries were sited outside the protection of the Singapore anti-aircraft defences, though some 40mm LAA guns were initially deployed to protect both Buona Vista and Johore Batteries. As the battle for the Island developed, a number of the coastal batteries were to suffer as a result of air attack.

The Japanese opened their ground attack on Singapore on 4 February with a heavy artillery bombardment. British counter-battery fire was limited, partly because of a restricted supply of 25pdr ammunition and partly because it was believed necessary to keep the gun positions concealed. However, on 5 February the guns of Johore, Tekong Besar and Sphinx Batteries fired on west Johore Bahru and the mainland north of Punggol Point. The next day, Tekong Besar and Sphinx batteries registered targets on Pulau Ubin and the mainland north of the Island.

The period from 4 to 8 February was used by the Japanese to regroup and prepare their forces for the final assault, which commenced on the night of 8/9 February. The plan was for the 5th and 18th Japanese Divisions to cross the Johore Strait west of the Causeway, part of which had been demolished by the British. Meanwhile, troop concentrations continued to be obvious to the east of the causeway, so confirming General Percival's conviction that the main enemy attack would come from the north-east.

Sphinx Battery in 1937, showing one of the 6in Mark XXIV counter-bombardment guns on a Central Pivot Mark V mounting. The tracks of the light railway that connected the batteries on Pulau Tekong Besar can be seen behind the gun position. (*TNA WO 252/1359*)

The Japanese attack struck the 22nd and 27th Australian Brigades, which were positioned on extended fronts made difficult to hold because of mangrove and creeks. The Japanese artillery barrage destroyed brigade and artillery communications, enabling their divisions to quickly secure bridgeheads on the north-west shore of the Island. In the early hours of 9 February the guns of Pasir Laba Battery engaged likely enemy embarkation points on the southern coast of Johore, firing forty rounds from No 1 gun. This gun had had part of its concrete anti-splinter protection removed to allow greater traverse, but the No 2 gun, which still had this protection in place, was unable to engage any targets. At 0700 hours the battery was attacked by numerous dive-bombers and heavily shelled by a Japanese battery; the battery observation post and the No 1 gun were destroyed and the overhead cover for the other gun smashed.

As a result, the HKSRA gunners manning the battery evacuated it, and orders were given for its demolition. The battery commander, Captain Asher RA, prepared the magazine for destruction but was unfortunately killed while assisting a casualty at the magazine entrance. The guns and the magazine were subsequently all destroyed by 1830 hours.

Interestingly, it would seem that Captain Asher may have acted on his own initiative in removing part of the concrete anti-splinter protection to improve the arc of fire. When Captain Thomas Pickard, commanding the AMTB guns at Batu Berlayer, requested permission from HQ Fixed Defences to cut away part of the wall of the gun emplacements to provide a limited arc of fire landwards, the reply he received was, 'It is not the policy of the CFD [Commander Fixed Defences] to sanction alteration to construction of War Office design'.[7] Rather a short-sighted decision in the circumstances, though it is doubtful if the guns would have been able to contribute much to the battle.

During the same night the enemy troop concentrations on the mainland north of Punggol Point that were fixing General Percival's attention were engaged by Johore, Tekong Besar and Sphinx Batteries.

By the evening of 10 February the defending forces had been forced back to a makeshift line stretching from Bukit Panjang to Pasir Panjang, but on the night of 10/11 February the Japanese smashed through it. Their attack carried them almost to Bukit Timah and appeared to threaten Buona Vista Battery, which had been prepared for demolition the previous day. At 0600 hours on 11 February the guns of the battery were destroyed by their gunners without having fired a shot in anger.

On the afternoon of 11 February the Japanese Imperial Guards Division was launched in a follow-up assault, crossing just east of the Causeway and landing almost unopposed, as the Australian 27th Brigade defending the area was in the process of withdrawing from its positions on the orders of the brigade commander. Advancing in conjunction with the 5th and 18th Japanese Divisions on the axis towards Panjang village and Bukit Timah, the Japanese now aimed to split the defending forces and capture the high ground overlooking the city, and the water supply.

The 44th Indian Brigade, which had been holding the defence positions on the south-west corner of the island, attempted with the remnants of the 22nd Australian Brigade to make a stand on the so-called 'Kranji–Jurong Line'. This line existed in name only and, to make things worse, the commander of 22nd Brigade misinterpreted General Percival's warning order regarding the holding of a 'last-ditch' perimeter around the city and withdrew prematurely to the perimeter, leaving a hole in the line.

Throughout 11 February those guns of the fixed defences that could bear on targets engaged the Japanese. Batteries of Changi Fire Command, Johore, Tekong Besar and Sphinx Batteries, fired at targets on the mainland, chiefly with armour-piercing shells which, while not doing much damage, did, according to Japanese sources, have considerable psychological effect! However, during the day Japanese aircraft attacked Johore Battery; no serious harm was done to the 15in guns of the battery, but the railway line connecting the guns with the Changi magazine was damaged.

In Faber Fire Command the three 9.2in guns of Fort Connaught engaged the Jurong River position and the village of Ulu Pandan. The guns of Fort Siloso and Labrador Battery engaged enemy troop concentrations on the west coast road and the Jurong River position; in turn, Fort Siloso was bombed by Japanese aircraft, but without serious damage to the guns.

A 9.2in Mark X BL gun on a Mark VII (35°) mounting. The photograph probably shows one of the guns of the battery on Pulau Tekong Besar. (*IWM K714*)

The battle for Singapore reached its climax on 12 February when General Percival ordered last-ditch counter-attacks against Japanese forces assaulting Bukit Timah. The guns of Fort Connaught put down concentrated fire on Tengah airfield, which the Japanese were using as a forming-up position, and on Bukit Timah, where two Japanese battalions supported by tanks were spearheading the assault. Johore Battery also engaged targets in the Bukit Timah area and the Pasir Panjang road, before these guns were destroyed by their gunners. Tekong Besar and Sphinx Batteries continued to engage targets on the Johore mainland.

Despite the spirited intervention of these batteries, 12 February was a grim day for the fixed defences. In addition to the destruction of Johore Battery, Changi Battery and the batteries at Beting Kusah and Changi Outer were all destroyed without their having taken any part in the battle, in order to prevent them from falling into Japanese hands in working condition. The remaining personnel of the batteries from 9th Coast Regiment RA were then formed into an infantry unit of four rifle companies.

The Japanese attacks on 12 February finally convinced General Percival and General Heath, the commander of III Indian Corps, to abandon the remaining coastal defences and withdraw the troops into a perimeter around the city. The formation of this final line involved the loss of the main store dumps and meant that rations were now down to a week's supply; ammunition stocks were also at a dangerously low level, and the abandoned coast batteries no longer provided the limited level of support they had previously.

On 13 February the guns of Fort Connaught continued to fire on Bukit Timah, while the Fort Siloso guns and Labrador Battery engaged targets on the west coast road. Labrador Battery was supporting the 1st Battalion the Malay Regiment (1 Malay) which was holding Pasir Panjang Ridge, high ground in the south-west of the island. The battalion held hastily constructed positions, reinforced by pillboxes on the coast road, and was the only major unit between the Japanese and the southern flank of the new perimeter.

At 1400 hours a Japanese 5.9in (150mm) battery shelled the Labrador Battery, damaging the observation post, the magazine and the overhead cover of No 2 gun. Three Indian other ranks were killed and six wounded.

A target in the Pasir Panjang area was engaged and this resulted in further Japanese counter-battery fire, causing the Indian gunners to take cover in the magazine of the old Fort Pasir Panjang nearby.

Fierce fighting was taking place on Pasir Panjang ridge, but despite dogged resistance, by dusk 1 Malay were unable to hold the Japanese attack, which reached Alexandra Road. On this being reported to Faber Fire Command, orders were given to complete the demolition of the fort, and the two guns, the magazine, searchlights and engine room were successfully destroyed. The battery personnel withdrew to Faber Fire Command and, as a consequence of the abandonment of Labrador Battery, the anti-motor torpedo boat battery at Berlayer Point was also demolished and the 18pdr QF gun at Pulau Hantu was destroyed.

The 6in counter-bombardment guns of Sphinx battery and the 12pdr QF gun of Ladang anti-motor torpedo boat battery continued to engage parties of Japanese troops on Pulau Ubin throughout 13 February, but there is no record of the Tekong Besar guns engaging the enemy on that day.

On the night of 13 February the guns of Serapong Battery and Fort Siloso fired on one of the very few naval targets to be engaged during the battle. There is some doubt as to the actual target, but Major C. C. M. Macleod-Carey, second-in-command of 7th Coast Regiment RA, who was in the Faber Fire Control Centre at the time, believed it to be a large Japanese troop carrier. However, the Fixed Defences War Diary, written after the fall of Singapore, refers only to a '*Tekong*', or barge, loaded with oil drums.

The end for the remaining batteries of the fixed defences came the following day, 14 February, a truly unhappy St Valentine's Day for the garrison. At 0500 hours, as a result of a false report that the Japanese had landed on Blakang Mati, the guns of Fort Siloso were destroyed; shortly afterwards, at 0715 hours, the guns of Fort Connaught were destroyed also. The destruction of the guns of the Serapong Spur 6in battery followed soon afterwards at midday. Twelve hours later, by 1830 hours, the remaining batteries of the fixed defences, Silingsing, Pengerang, Tekong Besar, Sphinx, Berhala Reping, Ladang, Calder Harbour and Sajahat, had all been destroyed by their gunners.

With the defence in disarray, a shortage of ammunition, the water supply to the city in the hands of the Japanese, heavy damage to the city and civilian casualties, General Percival was given permission by General Wavell to surrender to General Yamashita; the surrender occurred at 1715 hours on 15 February. Interestingly, it was not until a week later, on 22 February, that the Japanese finally occupied the Tekong Besar and Pengerang areas and mopped up the personnel of the two batteries.

Despite the myth that the guns of Singapore's fixed defences 'pointed the wrong way', it is fair to say that they fulfilled their deterrent role, since no attempt was made by the Japanese navy to attack the island from the sea. Indeed, some of the guns made a considerable contribution, despite the inadequate ammunition, to the defence of Singapore against attack by land.

Chapter 11

Aftermath: 1942–1956

As the Japanese advanced and threatened the majority of Singapore's fixed defences, steps were taken by the British garrison to render their guns unserviceable and deny them to the enemy. Most of the guns were either destroyed or put out of service by means of removing the breech blocks, sights, dials and other essential items. In the case of the Tekong Besar 9.2in (233mm) battery and the Serapong 6in (152mm) No 2 gun, the

Johore Battery No 2 15in gun destroyed by the British prior to the surrender of Singapore. Photographed in 1946. (*TNA WO 203/6034*)

positions were totally destroyed by detonating the magazines. A number of guns, including one of the Sejahat Twin 6pdr QF equipments, were put out of action by exploding rounds in the barrels, while the 15in (380mm) guns of Johore and Buona Vista Batteries were destroyed using gelignite charges. However, most guns were put out of action by the orthodox method of blowing out the breech screw.

It would appear that the Japanese were unable to make use of the captured guns and searchlights; indeed, only four guns (and three searchlights) were reported as being re-usable: one of the 15in BL guns at Buona Vista Battery;

12pdr QF gun mounted in a Twin 6pdr QF equipment position at Oso AMTB battery adjacent to Fort Siloso. This gun was one of the four maintained by the Japanese. (*TNA WO 203/6034*)

two 6in BL guns, one from Beting Kusah Battery and one from Labrador Battery; and the 12pdr QF gun from Oso, the AMTB battery at Fort Siloso. The Buona Vista Battery gun was found to have a shell in the barrel, which the Japanese removed, and a subsequent British intelligence report stated that the gun was still in use; but as the mechanical loading system had been destroyed, the gun had to be loaded and operated manually. The Japanese report on the Singapore guns noted that the Beting Kusah and Labrador 6in guns could be made operational again by using spare breech blocks and other spare parts, although the bores were rusted and required cleaning.[1]

There is, however, some mystery regarding the 12pdr QF gun mounted in the empty Twin 6pdr QF position at Fort Siloso. According to the battery commander, the gun was disposed of by dropping it over the cliff into the sea. However, the Japanese appear to have recovered the gun, refurbished it and remounted it in its old position. The Japanese also reported capturing forty-nine searchlights, a total that appears to have included sixteen beach defence lights, though only eight of these were considered to be repairable locally, together with sixteen engines.[2]

Despite refurbishing these guns, it would appear that the Japanese made little use of them. In a report on the Japanese plans for the defence of Singapore compiled by the British after the Japanese surrender it was stated that the guns at Beting Kusah and Buona Vista were never fired because there were no gun crews who knew how to operate them.[3] This would seem to be another underestimation of the ability of the Japanese military; it is more likely that these guns were never fired because the Japanese did not take the problem of defending Singapore seriously until the end of July 1945.

In Japanese eyes the significance of Singapore was reduced simply to a question of prestige, and it was low on the priority list for equipment and reinforcements. The major Japanese formation on the island was the Singapore Garrison Unit, with a strength of approximately 2,000 officers and men. The Japanese plan for the defence of Singapore would appear to have been based on a series of 'fortresses' of battalion strength, made up from rear echelon troops, located on commanding features and sited to control main roads and other vulnerable points. A centrally located counter-attack force, probably drawn from the Garrison Unit, would be committed once the main British effort became apparent.

A small number of Japanese 140mm and 150mm guns were mounted in a coast defence role, with one 150mm and one 140mm gun sited on a hill south of Changi Point, and another 140mm gun at Tanjong Pengelih, east of Pengerang on the Johore mainland. Two 140mm guns were also sited at Nee Soon in the centre of the Island, with the role of landward defence. Only one new concrete casemate was found after the British reoccupied Singapore, and that was for a smaller 120mm gun.[4] Subsequently, a number of Japanese guns which had not been discovered by the British Army were unearthed. Two 150mm guns were found in 1966 buried in the Mandai jungle south-west of Sembawang near the Kranji war cemetery, and four 120mm 45 calibre dual-purpose guns were uncovered in the vicinity of the Upper Pierce reservoir in the early 1970s. These guns can now be seen in the Fort Siloso Military Museum.

Little effort was made by the Japanese to improve the beach defences, which in 1945 were in very poor condition. No new pillboxes were constructed, but a number of bunker complexes made of earth and timber were set up inland on areas of high ground to form redoubts.

With the reoccupation of Singapore at the end of 1945 it was necessary to inspect what remained of the British fixed defences, evaluate their potential for future use and make recommendations on the future defence requirements of the Island. Colonel F. W. Rice was sent from the War Office in London to inspect the fixed defences of both Singapore and Hong Kong and draw up proposals regarding their restoration.

Colonel Rice confirmed that the majority of pre-war fixed defences were no longer useable and that most of the guns had only scrap value. His report stated that 'every gun of the original twenty-four batteries in Singapore is out of action for reasons varying from complete disintegration as in the case of Tekong Besar No 2 gun, to the deficiency of minor parts as in the case of the No 2 gun at Buona Vista Battery'.[5] In addition, a large amount of ammunition was still to be found in the undamaged magazines. However, Colonel Rice did identify the two 6in BL guns and the 15in BL gun salvaged by the Japanese as being serviceable, and recommended that the 15in gun should be overhauled, repaired and placed in a state of care and maintenance. The other 6in 15° batteries he declared to be obsolescent, and he recommended that they should not be restored.

One of the Twin 6pdr QF equipments of the Sejahat AMTB battery destroyed by its gun crew on 15 February 1942. Photographed in 1946. (*TNA WO 203/6034*)

For the future defence of the naval base and the commercial harbour Rice proposed a short-term defence plan that provided for the re-establishment of the two Fire Commands, Changi and Faber, each controlling one counter-bombardment battery, one examination battery and two or three AMTB batteries. In the Changi Fire Command the counter-bombardment battery was to be the restored Sphinx Battery, armed with three 6in Mark XXIV BL guns; Beting Kusah Battery, armed with the old 6in Mark VII guns, was to act as the examination battery; and the AMTB batteries were to be at Changi Outer (Palm) and Pulau Sejahat, each with two Twin 6pdr QF equipments.

Faber Fire Command was to have the guns of Fort Connaught as its counter-bombardment battery, with three 9.2in Mark X BL guns; Silingsing was to be the examination battery; and the AMTB batteries, each equipped with two Twin 6pdr QF equipments, were to be at Batu Berlayer, Berhala Reping and Tanjong Tereh.

In order to provide some form of immediate defence for Singapore the decision was taken in March 1946 to instal the two remaining serviceable 6in BL guns in Fort Siloso. These guns would initially act as an examination battery, and were to be manned by the newly formed 1st Singapore Coast Battery RA. The personnel of the new battery was to comprise British officers and senior NCOs and Malay other ranks, and in August of the same year it was renamed the 1st Malay Coast Battery RA.

The guns were installed in the existing emplacements in the fort, but without range-finders, transmitting and receiving dials, gun telescopes or telephones. Nor was any fire control equipment provided, until the arrival of a Fire Direction Table in late 1947, so to all intents and purposes the guns were not operational.

The Chiefs of Staff Committee considered the defences of Singapore at a meeting held on 18 December 1947, at which the Admiralty representative stated that defences were required for both entrances to the Strait of Johore in order to protect the naval dockyard and anchorage. Defences would also be required for the protection of the commercial anchorage and the main port of Singapore. The committee minuted that the 'current' defences in Singapore were five 6in Mark VII BL guns and eleven Twin 6pdr QF equipments.[6] This can only refer to the proposed armament, as at that date only the two guns mentioned in the previous paragraph were actually mounted. However, in January 1948 a single Twin 6pdr QF equipment was transferred from Ceylon (Sri Lanka), where it had been mounted in the Colombo Breakwater Battery, and mounted in the old Oso position at Fort Siloso. The mounting of this equipment was complete by March 1948.

By the end of the 1940s the whole concept of coast defence in Britain and the Empire was under severe scrutiny, at a time when there was intense pressure to reduce spending on defence. It was clear by the end of the Second World War that the battleship no longer reigned supreme; it had now been superseded in its role as 'Queen of the Sea' by the aircraft carrier. Air power now dominated naval operations, added to which there was now no obvious enemy naval power. With the demise of the Japanese navy the danger to Singapore had been removed, and any threat from the Soviet Union had still to develop. As a result, the policy on coastal defence was reviewed and the decision taken that there was now no naval threat that would justify the replacement of guns heavier than 6in.

In 1950 the two recovered 6in guns at Fort Siloso were replaced with three more modern 6in Mark XXIV BL guns on Mark V mountings. These came from the Stella Maris Battery at Haifa, and two were mounted in Fort Siloso, while the third was retained as a reserve and training gun elsewhere in the fort. The Central Pivot Mark II gun pits were modified to take the new Mark V mountings, and improvements were carried out to the structure of the battery, including the renovation of the magazine, the construction of a position-finding cell and the moving underground of the engine room.

In the same year, two further Twin 6pdr QF equipments were dispatched to Singapore, one of which also came from Haifa; one was mounted in the

One of the three 6in Mark XXIV BL Guns on Mark V mountings installed in Fort Siloso in 1950. (*Author's collection*)

old wartime battery positions at Batu Berlayer Point, opposite Fort Siloso, and the other in Berhala Reping on Blakang Mati. At the same time, the name of the 1st Malay Coast Battery RA was changed to become D Coast Artillery Cadre Battery RA.

Because of the development of ballistic and guided missiles as weapons of war, the sub-committee for Air, Coast and Seaward Defence of the Chiefs of Staff Committee continued to review the use of guns for coastal defence. Radar was now the main means of range-finding, and the Radar Coast Artillery Number 2 Mark I equipment was now the standard range-finder in use by coastal batteries. One such radar was installed at Mount Serapong on Blakang Mati to control the fire of the new 6in Mk XXIV guns at Fort Siloso. The sub-committee also recommended the use of guns for other than their designated roles: the 3.7in (94mm) HAA gun was given a mobile coast defence role, while instructions were given that all Twin 6pdr QF equipments were to be modified for anti-aircraft firing.[7]

In 1951 the decision was taken by the Chiefs of Staff Committee that the role of counter-bombardment was to be assumed by the Royal Navy, and the coast artillery roles were to be limited to support of the Examination Service, Anti-Small Battle Unit defence and closure of straits.[8] This was the beginning of the end for coast defence generally. On 17 February 1956 the Minister of Defence, Sir Walter Monckton, announced in the House of Commons that coastal artillery was to be abolished. In the light of modern weapon development, the government believed that there was no longer any justification for maintaining coastal artillery, and so all existing units were to be disbanded or converted to new roles. In May 1956 the disbandment of all overseas coast defence was announced, and on 31 December 1956 coast artillery in Britain and overseas, including Singapore, ceased to exist.

The fortifications today

In 2015 it is difficult to imagine Singapore as a heavily fortified military base. Today it is a huge, bustling, immensely prosperous metropolis. Urban development and land reclamation have steadily caused most of the battery sites on the main island to disappear, including all the early Victorian batteries with the exception of portions of Fort Pasir Panjang. As a result of the construction of a large underground municipal reservoir on the top of Fort Canning Hill by the city council between 1923 and 1927 nothing remains of the old Fort Canning except the main gate.

The huge Buona Vista and Johore Batteries have both disappeared; Buona Vista as a victim of urban development, and Johore subsumed into Changi International Airport. In the case of the latter, however, a replica 15in gun has been built on the site of the old No 1 gun position as a memento of the huge guns that were once sited there.

The only other remains of batteries still visible on Singapore Island itself are those of Labrador Battery and parts of the old Fort Pasir Panjang, together with the Batu Berlayer AMTB battery and the foundations of one of the caponiers of Fort Tanjong Katong. The remains of Labrador Battery are in Labrador Park, where a number of gun positions can still be seen, together with the old magazine, though the latter is not open to the public. The remains of the Batu Berlayer battery are to be found on the headland at the beach entrance to Labrador Park. The gun position and fire control tower of the post-war battery remain, but access is difficult as the site is secured with a high steel fence.

The foundations of one of the caponiers of Fort Tanjong Katong were discovered in what is now Tanjong Katong Park as the result of an archaeological excavation carried out in 2004/5. After the foundations had been photographed and recorded the excavation was filled in, leaving only the outline of the top of the caponier's foundation, and this is now protected by low metal railings which allow visitors to view the site.

The other remains of Singapore's defences are to be found on Blakang Mati, now renamed Sentosa Island, on some of the outlying islands and at Pengerang on the Johore mainland. Sentosa Island is now a resort operated by the Sentosa Development Corporation. They have restored much of Fort Siloso at the northern end of the island, and it is now a military museum open to the public with a large display of historic guns. Throughout the island the corporation have also restored and re-used numerous old British military buildings.

Elsewhere on Sentosa it is possible to see substantial remains of the battery on Mount Imbeah, and of Fort Serapong, though the latter is now almost totally overgrown with vegetation. At Fort Connaught the emplacement for

The remains of Batu Berlayer AMTB battery can still be seen at Bath Berlayer Point. The photograph shows the director tower and part of one of the gun positions. (*Author's photograph*)

No 3 gun still exists, with its magazine; however, this gun position is now in the grounds of the Tanjong golf course and surrounded by vegetation. The remains of the battery at Pengerang are now similarly overgrown, and the gun positions are within the grounds of a Royal Malaysian Navy establishment.

Substantial elements of a number of AMTB batteries are still to be found by the intrepid investigator. On Berhala Reping, which was a small island off the south-east tip of what is now Sentosa Island and which, as a result of land reclamation, is now part of the Serapong golf course on Sentosa, the

The Mount Imbeah 9.2in gun position as it is today within the Sentosa Island resort. (*Author's photograph*)

post-war gun position and director tower for the Twin 6pdr QF equipment are still visible. On Ladang, at the eastern entrance to the Strait of Johore, the gun position, a number of the battery buildings and the director tower remain within what is now a Singapore naval base.

Similarly, the remains of the AMTB battery on Pulau Ubin, Calder Harbour AMTB Battery and Pulau Sejahat AMTB Battery on Pulau Tekong Besar can still be seen. The battery on Pulau Ubin is now in the grounds of a scout camp. However, on Pulau Brani the Tanjong Tereh AMTB Battery has disappeared under what is now the Brani container port, and Changi Outer (Palm) Battery and Changi Inner (School) Battery have disappeared as a result of urban development around the airport.

A number of pillboxes still remain on Singapore and Sentosa Islands. In Singapore City a pillbox can be seen at the junction of Pasir Panjang Rd and Science Park Rd, with a second one on Labrador beach. On Sentosa Island a pillbox still remains on Siloso beach, with two more, now rather garishly painted, on Palawan beach. There is also a pillbox, covered in vegetation, at Pengerang.

It reflects well on the Government of Singapore and, in particular, on the Sentosa Development Corporation, that despite the ever-increasing demands of urban development and land reclamation both are prepared to acknowledge that Singapore's military past is an important part of the history of the state and not just an aspect of its colonial past that is best forgotten.

Appendix A

Gazetteer of Forts and Batteries

(Map references from Singapore Armed Forces Mapping Unit, Singapore 1:50,000, Topographical Map 2010)

Batu Berlayer AMTB Battery   **GR 248274**

Initially established in 1892 to cover the western minefield. Considerable remains of the battery are still to be found on the headland adjacent to Labrador Park, but access is restricted.

Armament:

1892	1 x 6pdr 7cwt QF gun
	1 x Gardner 0.450in (11.4mm) calibre machine gun
1898	2 x 6pdr 7cwt QF guns on RCE (Elastic Stand Frame) Mounting
c.1905	2 x Maxim 0.303in (7.7mm) calibre machine guns on Cone Mountings
1936	Installation of 2 x Twin 6pdr QF equipments authorized
1942	2 x 12pdr 12cwt QF guns in Twin 6pdr QF equipment emplacements
	Guns destroyed (14 February)
1950–6	1 x Twin 6pdr QF equipment

Berhala Reping AMTB Battery   **GR 292259**

Established in 1892 to defend the entrance to the Sinki Strait and the eastern minefield. The remains of the gun positions and director tower can still be seen today, incorporated, as a result of land reclamation, into the Serapong course of the Sentosa Golf Club on Sentosa Island.

Armament:

1892	1 x 6pdr 7cwt QF gun on RCE Mounting
	1 x Gardner 0.450in (11.4mm) calibre machine gun
1898	2 x 6pdr 7cwt QF guns on RCE Mountings

1906   2 x Maxim 0.303in (7.7mm) machine guns on Cone Mountings
1940 (Aug) 2 x 12pdr 12cwt QF guns
1941 (Dec) 2 x Twin 6pdr QF equipments
1942   Guns destroyed (14 February)
1950–56   1 x Twin 6pdr QF equipment

Beting Kusah Close Defence Battery   GR 471381

Construction of a close defence battery for two 6in (152mm) guns was authorized in 1936. The battery site has now disappeared under Changi International Airport.

Armament:

1938   2 x 6in Mk VII BL guns on Central Pivot Mk II (15°) Mountings
1942   (14 February) One gun destroyed and one partially destroyed (later made serviceable by the Japanese)

Buona Vista Counter-bombardment Battery   GR 212337

Construction authorized in 1933 of a counter-bombardment battery for two 15in (380mm) guns. Today the site of the battery is partly within the perimeter of the Singapore Police Key Installation Protective Service camp and partly in the grounds of the adjoining Pine Grove condominium in Clementi, Bukit Timah. All remains have been sealed and covered over.

Armament:

1939   2 x 15in Mk I BL guns on Mk II (Spanish) Mountings
1942   (11 February) One gun destroyed and one gun partially destroyed (later made serviceable by the Japanese)

Calder Harbour AMTB Battery   GR 406444

Construction of a battery for two Twin 6pdr QF equipments on Pulau Tekong Besar was authorized in 1936. Remains of the gun positions and director towers are now within the Singapore Army Fighting-in-Built-up-Areas (FIBUA) firing range, and access is restricted.

Armament:
1941 (Dec) 2 x Twin 6pdr QF equipments
1942   Guns destroyed (14 February)

Changi Close Defence Battery   GR 444414

Construction of a battery for two 6in close defence guns was recommended by the Gillman Commission in 1927 and completed in 1931. The Singapore Air Traffic Control Centre has now been built on the site of the battery.

Armament:
1931   2 x 6in Mk VII BL guns on Central Pivot Mk II (15°) Mountings
1942   Guns destroyed (12 February)

Changi Inner (School) AMTB Battery   GR 452414

Construction of a battery for two Twin 6pdr QF equipments was authorized in November 1937. All remains of the battery have disappeared as a result of urban development around Changi International Airport.

Never armed

Changi Outer (Palm) AMTB Battery   GR 466405

Construction of a battery for two Twin 6pdr QF equipments was authorized in November 1937. All remains of the battery have been demolished as a result of the construction of Changi International Airport.

Armament:
1941 (Dec) 2 x Twin 6pdr QF equipments
1942   Guns destroyed (12 February)

Fort Canning & Fort Canning South Battery   GR 294307

Construction of a citadel as a keep of last resort was authorized in 1856, and work commenced in 1859. Now a park, and nothing remains of the old fort except the main gate.

Armament:

1859	7 x 68pdr 95cwt SB guns (South Battery)
	2 x 13in (330mm) SB mortars (Fort Canning)
1867	7 x 68pdr 95cwt SB guns (South Battery)
	8 x 8in (203mm) SB shell guns (Fort Canning)
	2 x 13in SB mortars (Fort Canning)
1885	4 x 64pdr RML guns (South Battery)
	3 x 13in SB mortars (Fort Canning
1898	1 x 7in (177mm) 6.5 ton RML gun
1904	7in RML gun removed

Fort Connaught   GR 286254

Construction of an open earthwork battery on Mount Serapong on Pulau Blakang Mati was authorized by the Colonial Defence Committee in 1878. Initially, it was known as Blakang Mati East Battery, but in 1885 the decision was taken to build a permanent battery on the site of the old infantry redoubt. In 1890 the new fort was named Fort Connaught. Today the site of Fort Connaught is on Tanjong golf course on Sentosa Island. The remains of one gun emplacement, the magazine, Battery Observation Post, a fire control tower and plotting room can still be found, but are covered in undergrowth. Access to the site is limited.

Armament:

1878	3 x 7in 6.5 ton RML guns
	2 x 64pdr RML guns
1891	2 x 9.2in (233mm) Mk IV BL guns on Mk I Mountings
	3 x 7in 6.5 ton RML guns
1900	2 x 9.2in Mk IV BL guns on Mk I Mountings
	2 x 6in Mk II QF guns on Pedestal Mounting
1911	1 x 9.2in Mk X BL gun on Mk V (15°) Mounting
	2 x 9.2in Mk IV BL guns on Mk I Mountings
1913	1 x 9.2in Mk X BL gun on Mk V Mounting
1936–7	3 x 9.2in Mk X BL guns on Mk VII Mountings
1942	Guns destroyed (14 February)

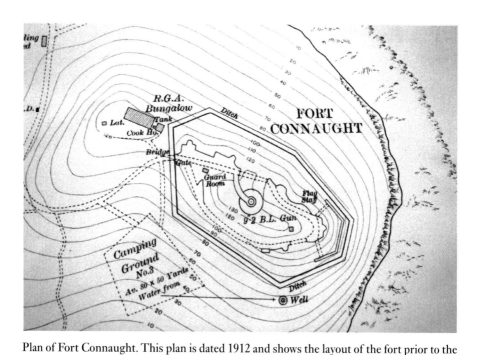

Plan of Fort Connaught. This plan is dated 1912 and shows the layout of the fort prior to the 1936 modernization. (*TNA WO 78/5373*)

Fort Faber   GR 268280

A Victorian battery constructed in 1855 and reported to be in a ruinous condition in 1878. Today there are no remains to be seen.

Armament:

1855	2 x 56pdr 98cwt SB guns
1869	Not armed
1878	2 x 8in SB shell guns proposed as a temporary measure, but it is uncertain if these were ever mounted

Fort Fullerton   GR 303299

First constructed in 1829 at the entrance to the Singapore River as an artillery redoubt. In 1858 it was reconstructed and re-armed. In 1876 the site was sold, and the Exchange Building and General Post Office were built there. A portion was retained for use as the drill hall of the Singapore Volunteer Artillery until 1904. All remains of Fort Fullerton are now beneath the old Fullerton Building, now the Fullerton Hotel.

Armament:

1829	Unknown
1858	3 x 56pdr 98cwt SB guns
	2 x 32pdr SB guns
1863	9 x 68pdr 95cwt SB guns
1871	9 x 68pdr 95cwt SB guns
1890	1 x 7in 6.5 ton RML gun (drill purposes)
1904	Gun removed

Fort Palmer   GR 295289

Initially constructed in 1855 on the lower slopes of Mount Palmer as a battery (Lake's), and rebuilt in 1890 to mount two 10in (254mm) BL guns. The fort was demolished in 1911 and Mount Palmer was levelled to fill and reclaim adjacent swamp land.

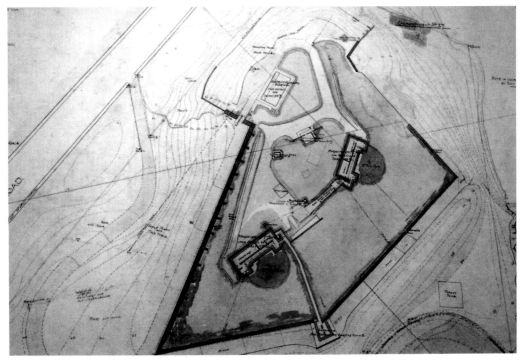

Plan of Fort Palmer in 1905 showing the positions for the two 10in (254mm) BL guns. (*TNA WO 78/5372*)

Armament:

1855	4 x 56pdr 98cwt SB guns
	1 x 8in SB shell gun
1864	5 x 56pdr 98cwt SB guns
1878	3 x 7in 6.5 ton RML guns
	2 x 64pdr RML guns
1890	2 x 10in Mk III BL guns on Carriage Garrison Barbette Mk I Mounting
1911	Guns removed

Fort Pasir Panjang   GR 247276

Constructed in 1878 on the direction of the Colonial Defence Committee to reinforce the defences of the western entrance to New Harbour. The fort was sited on a jungle-covered hillside and consisted of two gun positions, a gate and portcullis, with a road leading to the battery. A landing stage was provided for the delivery of ammunition, stores and personnel.

Armament:

1878	2 x 7in 6.5 ton RML guns
1886	3 x 7in 6.5 ton RML guns
1898	2 x 9.2in Mk IV BL guns on MK I Mountings
	1 x 7in 6.5 ton RML gun
1900	2 x 9.2in Mk IV BL guns on Mk I Mountings
	2 x 6in Mk II QF guns on Mk I Mountings
	2 x 6pdr 7cwt QF guns on RCE Mountings
1911	2 x 9.2in Mk IV BL guns on Mk I Mountings
	2 x Maxim machine guns on Cone Mountings
1913	Guns removed

Fort Serapong   GR 282259

In 1885 a battery was constructed on the site of an infantry redoubt at the summit of Mount Serapong on Blakang Mati. Two gun positions for BL guns were built. Considerable remains of the battery are still to be found, although very overgrown and difficult to access.

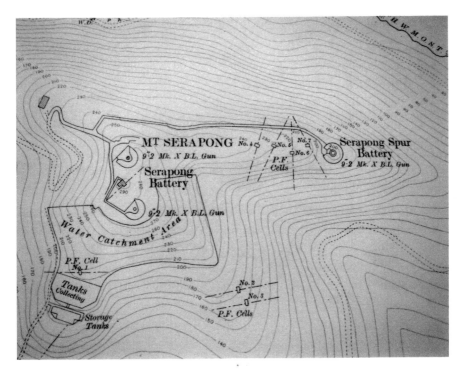

Plan of Fort Serapong and Serapong Spur Battery as completed to mount 9.2in (233mm) Mk X BL guns in 1908. (*TNA WO 78/4226*)

Armament:

1889	2 x 8in Mk VIIa BL Armstrong guns on Barbette Carriage Mk I
1908	8in guns removed
1911	2 x 9.2in Mk IV BL guns on Mk V (15°) Mountings
1936	Guns removed

Fort Silingsing   GR 281268

Battery constructed in 1899 on Pulau Brani, initially for two 12pdr QF guns, and known as Pulau Brani Battery. Silingsing Battery for two 6in Mk VII BL guns in the same location recommended by the Owen Committee, but two 6in QF guns actually mounted. These were replaced by 6in Mk VII BL guns in 1936. The battery was demolished during the 1973–4 land reclamation programme on Pulau Brani for the new container port.

Aerial photograph taken in the 1950s showing one of the Silingsing 6in (152mm) Mk VII CD battery gun positions. The arrow shows the site of the gun position. (*Lynne Copping*)

Plan of Fort Silingsing on Pulau Brani, 1912. (*TNA WO 78/5370*)

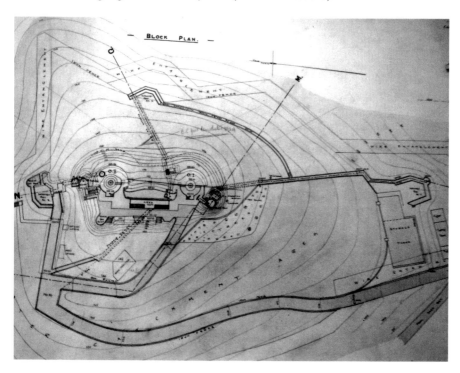

Armament:

1899	2 x 12pdr 12cwt QF guns
1907	Guns removed
1911	2 x 6in Mk II QF on Mk II Mountings
1936–7	2 x 6in Mk VII BL guns on Central Pivot Mk II (15°) Mountings
1942	Guns destroyed (14 February)

Fort Siloso   GR 252268

An earthwork battery position initially constructed 1878–82 on Blakang Mati and subsequently converted into a major fort with underground magazines, engine room, casemates, etc. In the twentieth century this battery became the Examination Battery for the Western Examination Anchorage. Today the fort is a military museum operated by the Sentosa Leisure Group.

Armament:

1878	3 x 7in 6.5 ton RML guns
	2 x 64pdr RML guns
1886	4 x 7in 6.5 ton RML guns
	2 x 64pdr RML guns
1887	4 x 7in 6.5 ton guns
1890	1 x 9.2in Mk IV BL gun on a Mk I Mounting
	4 x 7in 6.5 ton RML guns
1891	1 x 9.2in Mk IV BL gun on a Mk I Mounting
	2 x 7in 6.5 ton RML guns
1899	1 x 9.2in Mk IV BL gun on a Mk I Mounting
	2 x 6in Mk II QF guns on Mk 1 Mountings
	2 x 12pdr 12cwt QF guns on Mk I pedestal mounting
1907	1 x 9.2in Mk IV BL gun on a Mk I Mounting
	2 x 6in Mk II QF guns on Mk II Mountings
1909	9.2in gun removed
1933–6	2 x 6in Mk VII BL guns on Central Pivot Mk II (15°) Mountings
1942	Guns destroyed (14 February)
1950–6	3 x 6in Mk XXIV BL guns on Mark V Mountings

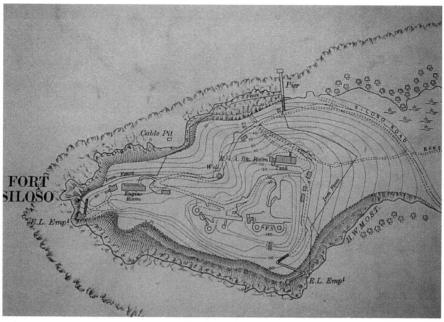

Plan of Fort Siloso dated 1912 showing the new positions for the 6in guns. (*TNA WO78/5369*)

Fort Tanjong Katong   **GR 335310**

Constructed in 1879 as a work *à fleur d'eau*. Primarily used as a training base for the Singapore Volunteer Artillery. The fort was demolished in 1901 and the foundations buried. After a recent archaeological excavation of the site, the outline of one of the three caponiers is to be seen at Tanjong Katong Park.

Armament:

1878	2 x 64pdr RML guns
1879	3 x 7in 7 ton RML guns
1889	2 x 8in Mk VIIa BL Armstrong guns on Barbette Carriage Mk I
1903	Guns removed

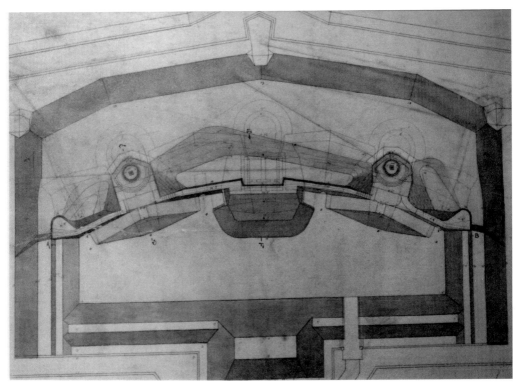

Plan of Fort Tanjong Katong as designed in 1885 for two 8in (203mm) BL Armstrong guns. The dotted outline shows the layout of the original fort, with the positions for the earlier 7in (177mm) 6.5 ton RML guns. (*TNA WO 78/4192*)

Fort Teregeh   GR 284265

A small battery constructed in 1887 on Pulau Brani to defend the minefield protecting the eastern entrance to Keppel Harbour and provided with three DELs. The fort has now disappeared as a result of the construction of the Pulau Brani container port.

Armament:

1887	2 x 7in 6.5 ton RML guns
1890	2 x 64pdr RML guns
1891	2 x 6pdr 22cwt QF guns
	2 x 64pdr RML guns

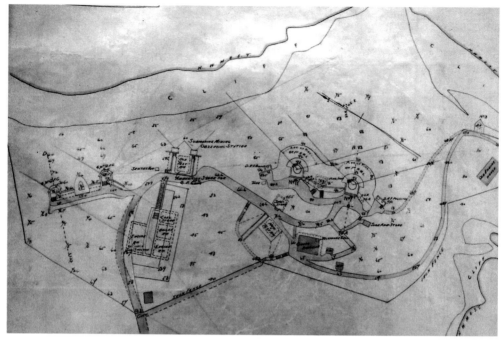

Plan of Fort Teregeh on Pulau Brani in 1896, showing the positions of both the older 64pdr RML guns and the later 6pdr QF guns. (*TNA WO 78/5371*)

1900	2 x 6pdr 7cwt QF guns
1907	4 x Maxim 0.303 in (7.7mm) machine guns on Cone Mountings
1939	1 x Twin 6pdr QF equipment proposed but not mounted

Johore Counter-bombardment Battery   GR 444389

In 1927 the Webb Gillman Commission recommended the installation of two 15in (380mm) BL guns at Bee Hoe, and in 1933 approval was given for the construction of a three-gun battery, which was completed in 1938/9. Today all remains of the battery have been covered over, and much of the site is now within the perimeter of Changi International Airport. A replica gun has now been placed on the site of the original No 1 gun of the battery.

Armament:

1938	2 x 15in Mk I BL guns on Mk II (Spanish 45°) Mountings
	1 x 15in Mk I BL gun on a Mk I (Singapore 55°) Mounting
1942	Guns destroyed (12 February)

Labrador Close Defence Battery   **GR 247276**
In 1935 approval was given for the construction of the new Labrador close
defence battery on the site of the disused Fort Pasir Panjang. Today the
remains of the gun emplacements have been incorporated into Labrador
Park, together with the 1892 magazine and casemates of Fort Pasir Panjang,
which are currently closed to the public.

Armament:

1937   2 x 6in Mark VII BL guns on Central Pivot Mk II (15°) Mountings
1942   (13 February) One gun destroyed and one damaged (subsequently
        made serviceable by the Japanese)

Ladang AMTB Battery   **GR 503433**
Authority was given in 1936 for the construction of a battery for one Twin
6pdr QF equipment at Ladang on Pulau Tekong Besar. Today the director
tower and gun emplacement remain in the grounds of the Singapore Army
Basic Military Training Centre.

Armament:

1938   Gun emplacement constructed
1941   1 x 12pdr 12cwt QF gun mounted in Twin 6pdr equipment
        emplacement
1942   Gun destroyed (14 February)

Lake's Battery (*see* Fort Palmer)

Mount Imbeah Battery   **GR 261265**
In 1910 the battery for one 9.2in BL gun, recommended by the Owen
Committee in 1906, was formally approved for construction on the site of the
infantry redoubt at Mount Imbeah, on Pulau Blakang Mati. Considerable
remains of the battery can still be found.

Armament:

1913   1 x 9.2in Mk X BL gun on Mk V (15°) Mounting
1937   Gun removed

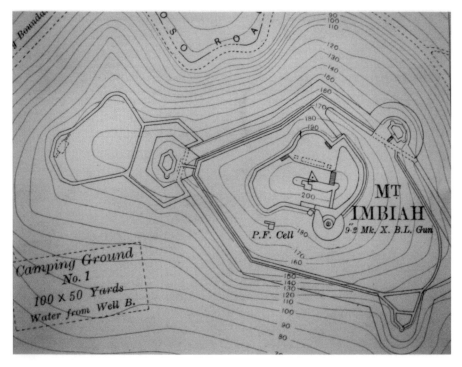

Plan of Mount Imbeah Battery in 1896, showing the position for the single 9.2in Mk X BL gun. (*TNA WO 78/5368*)

Oso (Siloso Point) AMTB Battery   **GR 251269**

Authority was given in 1936 for the construction of a battery for one Twin 6pdr QF equipment at Siloso Point on Pulau Blakang Mati. Today a replica 12pdr QF gun, the Twin 6pdr QF equipment emplacement and the director tower remain as part of the Fort Siloso military museum on Sentosa Island

Armament:

1938–9   Gun emplacement constructed
1941   1 x 12pdr 12cwt QF gun mounted in the Twin 6pdr QF emplacement
1942   Gun destroyed (14 February)

Pasir Laba Close Defence Battery   **GR 067376**

In 1927 the Webb Gillman Commission recommended strong defences for Pasir Laba, including 9.2in BL counter-bombardment guns and 6in BL close defence guns, to reinforce the defence of the western entrance to the Johore Strait. Construction of a battery of 6in Mk VII BL guns was authorized in 1936. The site of the gun emplacements are now on Singapore Ministry of Defence land, and some remains of the battery are believed to exist.

Armament:

1936   2 x 6in Mk VII BL guns on Central Pivot Mk II (15°) Mountings

1942   Guns destroyed (9 February)

Pengerang Close Defence Battery   GR 562383

Constructed in 1938–9 for two 6in BL guns, it was the only close defence battery built on the Johore mainland to defend Singapore. The remains of the gun emplacements are now within the perimeter of a Royal Malaysian Navy base. However, various battery buildings and a pillbox can be found near the ferry pier, though they are all considerably overgrown with jungle vegetation and difficult to access.

Armament:

1939   2 x 6in Mk VII BL guns on Central Pivot Mk II (15°) Mountings

1942   Guns destroyed (14 February)

Prince's (or Princess) Battery   GR 301295 (?)

A very early battery, situated on the shoreline approximately 250yds (230m) south of the mouth of the Singapore River, shown on a map of 1843. It is uncertain if the armament shown below, which was to replace older smooth-bore guns, was ever mounted. The site of the battery has now been built over.

Armament:

1859   3 x 68pdr 95cwt SB guns (proposed)
         2 x 8in SB shell guns (proposed)

Pulau Hantu (Keppel) AMTB Battery   GR 255274

Construction of a battery for one Twin 6pdr QF equipment on Pulau Hantu was authorized in 1936 but not carried out. A temporary gun position for a single gun was established in 1942. Pulau Hantu has now been subsumed within the Jurong Island port.

Armament:

1942	1 x 18pdr Mk IV field gun on a Hogg & Paul Platform (January)
	Gun destroyed (14 February)

Pulau Sejahat AMTB Battery   GR 488426

Construction of a battery for two Twin 6pdr QF equipments on Pulau Sejahat was authorized in 1936. Until recently, considerable remains of the battery were to be found. However, Pulau Sejahat is now connected to Pulau Tekong Besar, is within the perimeter of a military training base and is not open to the public.

Armament:

1941	2 x Twin 6pdr QF equipments
1942	Guns destroyed (14 February)

Pulau Ubin AMTB Battery   GR 435445

Construction of a battery for two Twin 6pdr QF equipments on Pulau Ubin was authorized in 1936. Battery emplacements and buildings were completed in 1940. The remains of the battery are still to be seen close to the scout camp on the north side of the island.

Never armed

Scandal Point Battery   GR 302304 (?)

Believed to be the earliest battery to be constructed in Singapore. Sited on a small knoll on the sea side of the 'English Church', now St Andrew's Anglican Cathedral. No remains of the battery exist today, as the sea wall and esplanade were built over the site in 1890.

Armament:

1820	6 x 12pdr SB guns (?)
1851	Battery dismantled

Serapong Spur Battery   GR 283258

Construction of a battery for one 9.2in BL gun on a spur of Mount Serapong on Pulau Blakang Mati was authorized in 1908, and the battery was operational in 1912. Little remains of the original emplacement as this was converted to mount a 6in Mk VII BL gun of the later Serapong Spur 6in close defence battery, constructed in 1936.

Armament:

1912   1 9.2in Mk X BL gun on Mk V (15°) Mounting

c.1936   Gun removed

Serapong Spur 6in Close Defence Battery   GR 283258

As a result of the Barron Report in 1935, a battery of two 6in close defence guns was built on the site of the old Serapong Spur 9.2in battery. The old 9.2in gun position was converted for one 6in gun, and the second 6in emplacement was constructed nearby.

Armament:

1938   2 x 6in Mk VII guns on Central Pivot Mk II (15°) Mountings

1942   Both guns destroyed (14 February)

Sphinx Counter-bombardment Battery   GR 364422

In 1931 a battery of two 6in counter-bombardment guns was proposed for a site on Pulau Tekong Besar, and construction was authorized in 1936. The battery is now on Singapore Ministry of Defence land and no remains are believed to exist.

Armament:

1938   2 x 6in Mk XXIV BL guns on Mk V (45°) Mountings

1942   Guns destroyed (14 February)

Tanjong Tereh AMTB Battery   GR 284265

Construction of a battery for one Twin 6pdr QF equipment and one DEL on Pulau Brani was authorized in 1936. The gun emplacement was completed and sited just below Fort Silingsing. No remains are now visible, as the battery site has disappeared under the Pulau Brani container port.

Never armed

Tekong Besar Counter-bombardment Battery   GR 377425
In 1927 the Webb Gillman Commission recommended that a battery of 6in (152mm) BL guns should be installed on Pulau Tekong Besar. In 1933 the Committee of Imperial Defence authorized the construction of a 9.2in gun battery on the island. The remains of some of the battery may still be seen, but they are now on Singapore Ministry of Defence land and not accessible to the public without permission.

Armament:

1937	3 x 9.2in Mk X BL guns on Mk VII Mountings
1942	Guns destroyed (14 February)

Teregeh Point Battery   GR 283267
A gun platform was established here in 1861, but there is no indication as to what guns were mounted. In 1888 two 64pdr RML guns were mounted in a battery position. In 1896 a new battery position for two 6pdr QF Hotchkiss guns was established just north of the old 64pdr RML battery, and in 1901 three DELs were installed.

Armament:

1888	2 x 64pdr RML guns
1896	2 x 6pdr 7 cwt QF guns
1913	Guns removed

Artillery Guns and Mortars in Use in Singapore: 1819–1956

Smooth-Bore

Type	Weight* (cwt)	Length (ft)	Calibre (ins)	Range (yds)	Comments
(Guns)					
56pdr	98.00	11.00	7.56	2,260	at 5° elev.
68pdr	95.00	10.80	8.12	3,000	
Shell Gun					
8in	65.00	9.00	8.05	1,920	at 5° elev.
(Mortar)					
13in Land Service	37.25	3.67	13.00	690–2,900	Range at 45° with varying charges. Wt of shell 200lb
Rifled Muzzle-loading					
64pdr	64.00	9.80	6.39	4,000	
64pdr	71.00	10.22	6.30	3,000	
7in 7 ton	140.00	12.50	7.00	3,000	effective range
7in 6.5 tons	130.00	11.00	7.00	3000	effective range
Quick-firing					
6pdr	7.25	8.13	2.24	7,500	Hotchkiss
12pdr	12.00	10.30	3.00	8,000	
Twin 6pdr	10.00	9.00	2.24	11,300	
6in QF	131.00	20.77	6.00	10,900	

Type	Weight* (cwt)	Length (ft)	Calibre (ins)	Range (yds)	Comments
Breech-loading (Tons)					
6in Mk VII Central Pivot Mtg Mk II (15%)	7.50	23.26	6.00 (152mm)	12,000– 19,700	Wt of shell 100lb Range dependent on ammunition
6in Mk XXIV on Mtg Mk V (45°)	7.50	23.26 (152mm)	6.00	24,500	at 45°
8in Mk VIIa on Central Pivot Mtg	11.50	19.25	8.00 (203mm)	9,000	Armstrong. Wt of shell 210lbs
9.2in Mk IV on Mtg Mk I (15°)	23.00	25.85	9.20 (233mm)	16,000	Wt of shell 380lbs
9.2in Mk X on Mtg Mk V (35°)	28.00	36.86	9.20 (233mm)	29,000	at 35°
10in MkIII on Mtg Mk IV (15°)	29.00	21.84	10.00 (254mm)	11,500	Wt of shell 500lbs
15in Mk on Mk II Mtg (45°)	1100.00	54.16	15.00	42,000	Wt of shell 1,938lbs

* Barrel Weight

Appendix C

Fire Control Equipment

With the old smooth-bore guns, fire control in the forts and batteries that defended a harbour or coastline was the responsibility of each gun captain, as it was on board a man-of-war in Nelson's time. However, the increased range of the new rifled guns required a more sophisticated form of control. Initially, guns were controlled by an officer in an observation post who observed the fall of shot and passed corrections to the guns by various methods, including speaking tube, megaphone or mechanical indicator.

This simple form of fire control was still essentially inaccurate, since it relied upon the officer in the observation post estimating the range to the target by eye. There was an urgent need for a more accurate system, and between 1870 and 1880 trials were carried out on a number of range-finding devices. Most required two observers spaced widely apart and using instruments to measure the two base angles of the triangle formed by the two observers and the target. This system required a piece of flat ground up to 440yds (400m) wide, something it was often very difficult to find in close proximity to a fort or battery, particularly on the coast.

It was Captain H. S. S. Watkin RA in the 1880s who produced a practical solution to the problem, when he realized that if the observer was above the waterline this height became the base of the measuring triangle. So a measurement of the angle of depression to the bow-waterline of the target automatically gave the range. The Watkin Depression Range-finder became standard equipment in every coastal fort and battery, with the information it provided being relayed to the guns by means of an electric telegraph.

A further problem that faced the gunners was the fact that a target ship was moving, so a method had to be devised to compute the amount the gun should be 'laid-off' to ensure that the shell would hit the target. Once again, Captain Watkin came up with an answer by developing his Depression

Position Finder. This equipment comprised a telescopic sight linked to a plotting table and an electrical transmission system.

The position finder was installed in a protected concrete bunker known as a 'cell', which was sited some distance from the guns and manned by trained observers. One of the observers kept the sight trained on the target, while the other used the plotter to predict the time of flight of the shell. With the position finder it was not necessary for the officer on the gun position to make a correction for displacement, but using the depression range-finder a displacement scale was needed, and the officer had continually to correct the ranges given to the dials.

Perhaps the greatest advantage of the position finder over the basic range-finder was that the former did not have to be placed close to the guns, while the latter did. Indeed, using the position finder to lay the guns meant that targets could be engaged which were actually invisible to the guns, and the observer at the position finder could, if necessary, fire the guns. By the turn of the century the Watkin position finders and range-finders were being installed in coast defence forts and batteries throughout the United Kingdom and overseas in the Dominions and colonies. Position finders were provided for batteries armed with 9.2in (233mm) BL guns and heavier weapons, and depression range-finders for batteries mounting 6in (152mm) BL guns and practice batteries.

Batteries were also frequently provided with Barr & Stroud optical range-finders, particularly where the battery was constructed to meet emergency defensive requirements, as in the Second World War. The most common model supplied was the 12ft (3.17m) range-finder. This consisted of two telescopes mounted in a common frame, with an eyepiece in the middle of the frame. When measuring the range, the range-finder itself formed the base of a triangle having at its apex the object, the range of which was determined by measuring the parallax. Invented in 1882, the Barr & Stroud range-finder used the 'coincidence' system to obtain the range to the target. In this system, the field of view is divided into two parts by a fine line, and the range to the object is obtained by bringing the image of the object on one side of the dividing line into exact coincidence with the corresponding image on the other side.

The position finders, depression range-finders and Barr & Stroud range-finders were best suited to engaging relatively slow moving targets at medium to long range. Indeed, there were considerable problems in engaging targets as a result of the increasingly longer ranges of the modern rifled heavy guns mounted on battleships. The Barr & Stroud FT24 15ft (4.6m) range-finder was accurate to 20,000yds (18,460m), while the enormous FZ 100ft (30m), which was installed in Singapore, was accurate to within 17yds (15.7m) at 31,000yds (28,615m). Beyond those ranges, accurate control of gunfire had to rely on spotting aircraft.

When the fire of counter-bombardment guns was controlled centrally, as it was in Singapore from the Fortress Command Posts at Changi and Mount Faber and from the position finding cells on Mount Faber and Pasir Panjang ridge, the bearing and range could be passed to the guns electrically by means of what was, at that time, the highly secret MAGSLIP automatic transmission system.

There were also problems in engaging fast-moving torpedo boats and destroyers, since the speed of the target meant there was very little time for the guns to range. At relatively short ranges what was known as the auto-sight could be used with the 4.7in (120mm) and 6in QF guns and the 6in BL gun. This sight, when laid on the bow-waterline of the target, automatically laid the gun for range and elevation.

However, the smaller 6pdr and 12pdr QF guns continued to be aimed by the gun layer, using a telescopic sight fitted to the mounting of the gun. In the case of the Twin 6pdr QF equipment, two gun layers controlled the guns using telescopic sights, one aiming for line and the other for elevation. The No 1 gun layer had a control that allowed him to converge the left-hand gun so that its shots struck in the same place as those of the right-hand gun at whatever range was being engaged.

After the Second World War the remaining coast defence batteries were equipped with mobile radar equipment. This was the Equipment Radar AA No 3 Mk 2/7 and it was used to provide both range and bearing to the target for the guns until the disbandment of Coast Artillery in 1956.

Notes

Archival Sources

TNA   The National Archives, Kew
SNA   Singapore National Archives
OIOC   British Library Oriental and India Office Collection
REL   RE Library
RAML   RA Museum & Library, 'Firepower'
NAI   National Archives of India
OUP   Oxford University Press
JMBRAS   Journal of the Malaysian Branch of the Royal Asiatic Society

Chapter 1: The Founding of Singapore

1. Crawfurd, John, *Journal of an Embassy to the Courts of Siam & Indo-China* (London, 1830), pp. 68–73.
2. Glendinning, Victoria, *Raffles and the Golden Opportunity* (London, Profile Press, 2012), p.144.

Chapter 2: The Early Fortifications 1819–1869

1. Wurtzburg, Charles Edward, *Raffles of the Eastern Isles*, (Oxford University Press, Singapore, 1954).
2. Letter from Colonel Nahuijs 1824 JMBRAS Vol XLII Pt 1, 1969, p.70.
3. Garrison Orders 1826–7, 20 Feb 1827 quoted in Harfield, Alan, *British and Indian Armies in the East Indies*, (Chippenham, Picton Publishing, 1984).
4. OIOC, IOR/F/4/1281/51422.
5. Ibid.
6. Harfield, Alan, *British and Indian Armies in the East Indies*, (Chippenham, Picton Publishing, 1984), p.143.
7. SNA, Straits Settlements Records, W8 No.226, 11 August 1843.
8. OIOC, IOR/E/4/962/435.
9. Firbank, Col. L. T., 'A History of Fort Canning', (unpublished manuscript).
10. OIOC, IOR/E/4/807.
11. TNA, CO 273/2.
12. Ibid.
13. Ibid.
14. NAI, Extract from Letter No 5965, Fort William, 14 December 1857. Public Works Dept. 1858, Cons. 150–5. Quoted in Murfett, Miksic, Farrell & Chiang, *Between Two Oceans* (Singapore, Marshall Cavendish Editions, 1999), p.70.
15. OIOC, IOR/E/4/852/1005.
16. TNA, CO 273/2.
17. Ibid.

18. Cameron, John, *Our Tropical Possessions in Malayan India,* (London, Smith, Elder & Co, 1865), p.34.
19. TNA, CO 273/8/502–9.

Chapter 3: A Time of Change 1865–1890
1. TNA, WO 55/847.

Chapter 4: The First Rifled Guns 1870–1880
1. TNA CAB 7/1.
2. Ibid.
3. Ibid.
4. TNA WO 106/6330.
5. TNA CAB 7/1.
6. Ibid.
7. Ibid.
8. REL *Royal Engineers Journal* Vol. IV, 1880. Paper IV, pp. 3–57.
9. TNA CO 129/205.
10. Ibid.
11. B & LA & RO W/3946.

Chapter 5: Bureaucrats and Breech-loaders 1881–1900
1. TNA CO 537/46.
2. TNA CAB 11/128.
3. TNA CO 537/147.
4. TNA CO 273/178/14372.
5. WO 33/92.
6. TNA CO 537/47.
7. Ibid.
8. *Illustrated Naval & Military Magazine* Vol. III, No 13, July 1885, p.72.
9. TNA CO 129/205 & CO 273/137.
10. TNA WO 33/56.
11. TNA CO 273/178.

Chapter 6: The First World War 1914–1920
1. TNA CAB 16/1.
2. Ibid.

Chapter 7: Building the Base 1921–1929
1. TNA WO 196/7.
2. Ibid.

Chapter 8: Arming the Base 1923–1933
1. TNA CAB 16/63.
2. TNA WO 196/17.
3. TNA WO 106/132.
4. TNA CAB 16/63.
5. TNA 106/132.
6. TNA WO 196/24.

Chapter 9: The Approach of War 1934–1941
1. TNA WO 196/21.
2. TNA WO 196/14.
3. TNA WO 106/2555.
4. TNA WO 196/17.
5. TNA WO 78/5366.
6. Ibid.
7. REL Letters of Brigadier Charles Turner, M1480.
8. TNA WO 32/17539.
9. Ibid.
10. Ibid.
11. TNA WO 196/21.
12. RAML Wildey Papers, MD1156.
13. TNA CAB 36/4.
14. RAML Wildey Papers, MD1156.

Chapter 10: The Battle for Singapore
1. Hack, Karl and Blackburn, Kevin, *Did Singapore Have to Fall?* (London, Routledge, 2005), p.112.
2. TNA WO 172/176.
3. TNA WO 106/2522.
4. TNA WO 32/9366.
5. Simpson, Brig. Ivan, *Too Little Too Late*, (Kuala Lumpur, UMCB Publication, 1981), p.24.
6. Ibid., p.69.
7. TNA WO 361/379.

Chapter 11: Aftermath 1942–1956
1. Office of the Chief of Military History, US Dept. of the Army, *Report on the Installations and Captured Weapons, Java and Singapore*, www.cgsc.contentdtm.oclc.org.
2. Ibid.
3. TNA WO 208/1041.
4. Ibid.
5. TNA WO 203/6034.
6. TNA DEFE 5/6/266.
7. TNA WO 192/176.
8. TNA WO 32/11031.

Glossary

AMTB	anti-motor torpedo boat.
Barbette	position in which guns are mounted to fire over a parapet wall rather than through embrasures in the wall.
Bastion	a defence work projecting outwards from the main walls of a defended place.
BL	breech-loading.
BLC	breech-loading converted.
Caponier	covered passage constructed across, or projecting into, a ditch to provide sheltered communication across the ditch or to defend it.
Casemate	a bomb-proof vaulted chamber built in the ramparts of a fort to contain cannon, or to provide barrack accommodation.
CASL	coast artillery search light (term used post 1941).
CB	counter-bombardment.
CD	close defence.
Chase	The part of a gun barrel forward of the trunnions.
Chasehooped	the strengthening of a weak gun barrel by shrinking on additional hoops over the chase of the barrel.
CID	Committee of Imperial Defence.
CMB	coastal motor boat.
CO	Commanding Officer.
Counterscarp	outer wall or slope of a ditch.
DEL	defensive electric light (term used pre-1918 for searchlights).
DPF	depression position finder.
DRF	depression range finder.
Embrasure	opening in a parapet or wall through which a gun can be fired.
GHQ	General Headquarters.
Glacis	open slope extending from the ditch giving a clear field of fire to the defenders.
GOC	General Officer Commanding.
Gorge	rear, whether open or closed, of any defensive work.
Grillage	heavy framework of cross-timbering as foundation for building in treacherous soil.
HAA	heavy anti-aircraft.
HEIC	Honourable East India Company.
HKSRA	Hong Kong & Singapore Royal Artillery.
Holdfast	a steel plate secured into the ground by long vertical bolts sunk into a concrete base on which heavy guns in fixed positions were secured.
LAA	light anti-aircraft.

MNI	Madras Native Infantry.
Martello Tower	small circular tower, usually on the coast to prevent hostile landing.
Monitor	shallow-draught warship armed with heavy guns.
MTB	motor torpedo boat.
OC	officer commanding.
OP	observation post.
Parapet	stone breastwork designed to give defenders on a wall or tower protection from enemy fire and observation.
Pdr	abbreviation of 'pounder', referring to the weight of shell fired by the gun.
PF	position finder.
Pulau (Malay)	island.
QF	quick-firer.
RA	Royal Artillery.
Racer	circular or semi-circular horizontal metal rail along which the traversing platform of a heavy gun moved.
RBL	rifled breech-loading.
RCE	elastic stand frame for small quick-firing guns.
RE	Royal Engineers.
Redoubt	a small fortified work, standing alone without bastions, usually designed as an infantry stronghold.
RGA	Royal Garrison Artillery.
RML	rifled muzzle-loading.
SB	smooth-bore.
SL	searchlight.
Scarp	inner wall or slope of a ditch.
Terreplein	area on top of a rampart or tower and surrounded by a parapet where guns are mounted.
Traverse	a defensive barrier, usually a wall or earth bank, placed at right-angles to the main line of defence in order to protect the defenders from flanking fire.
VOC	Dutch East India Company.

Bibliography

Books

Allen, Louis, *Singapore 1941–42*, (London, Davis-Poynter, 1977)

Barber, Noel, *Sinister Twilight* (London, Fontana Books, 1970)

Buckley, C. B., *An Anecdotal History of Old Times in Singapore* (Oxford, Oxford University Press, 1984)

Costello, John, *The Pacific War* (London, Collins, 1981)

Coupland, Sir Reginald, *Raffles of Singapore* (London, Collins, 1946)

Crick, Timothy, *Ramparts of Empire: the Fortifications of Sir William Jervois Royal Engineer 1821–1897* (Exeter, The Exeter Press, 2012)

Elphick, Peter, *Singapore, the Pregnable Fortress – a Study in Deception, Discord and Desertion* (Edinburgh, Coronet Books, 1995)

Farrell, Brian P., *Defence and Fall of Singapore 1940–42*, (Stroud, Tempus, 2006)

Glendinning, Victoria, *Raffles and the Golden Opportunity* (London, Profile Books, 2012)

Grehan, John & Mace, Martin (eds), *Disaster in the Far East 1940–42* (Barnsley, Pen & Sword Books, 2015)

Grenfell, Russell, *Main Fleet to Singapore* (London, Faber & Faber, 1951)

Hack, Karl & Blackburn, Kevin, *Did Singapore Have To Fall: Churchill and the Impregnable Fortress* (London, Routledge, 2003)

Harfield, Alan, *British & Indian Armies in the East Indies (1685–1935)* (Chippenham, Picton Publishing, 1985)

Hill, C. A. G., *Singapore Old Strait & New Harbour*, in Bogaars, George, *The Tanjong Pagar Dock Co Ltd 1864–1905*, Memoirs of the Raffles Museum No 3, December 1956 (Singapore, Government Printing Office, 1956)

Hogg, I. V. & Thurston, L. F., *British Artillery Weapons & Ammunition 1914–1918* (London, Ian Allen, 1972)

Hughes, Maj Gen B. P. (ed), *History of the Royal Regiment of Artillery – Between the Wars 1919–39* (London, Brassey's UK, 1992)

Kirby, Maj Gen. S. Woodburn, *The War Against Japan, Volume I, The Loss of Singapore* (London, HMSO, 1959)

Makepeace, Brooke & Braddell (eds), *One Hundred Years of Singapore* (Singapore, Oxford University Press, 1991)

McIntyre, David, *The Rise and Fall of the Singapore Naval Base 1919–1942* (London, The Macmillan Press, 1979)

Maurice-Jones, Col K. W., *History of Coast Artillery in the British Army* (London, RA Institution, 1959)

Moor, J. H., *Notices of the Indian Archipelago and Adjacent Countries* (Singapore, 1837)

Moore, D. & J., *The First 150 Years of Singapore* (Singapore, Donald Moore Press, 1969)

Moss, Michael & Russell, Iain, *Range & Vision: The First Hundred Years of Barr & Stroud* (Edinburgh, Mainstream Publishing, 1988)

Murfett, Miksic, Farrell & Chiang, *Between Two Oceans: A Military History of Singapore from 1275 to 1971* (Singapore, Marshall Cavendish, 2011)

Parkinson, C. Northcote, *Britain in the Far East: the Singapore Naval Base 1909–1993* (Singapore, Donald Moore 1995)

Russell-Roberts, Denis, *Spotlight on Singapore* (Letchworth, Tandem Books, 1966)

Scholfield, Victoria, *Wavell: Soldier & Statesman* (London, John Murray, 2006)

Simpson, Brig Ivan, *Too Little Too Late* (London, Leo Cooper, 1970)

Singapore Artillery & Public Affairs Dept, *The Singapore Artillery 1888–1988* (Singapore, Ministry of Defence, 1988)

Smith, Colin, *Singapore Burning: Heroism and Surrender in World War II* (London, Viking, 2005)

Thompson, Peter, *The Battle for Singapore* (London, Portrait Books, 2005)

Thomson, John Turnbull, *Some Glimpses into Life in the Far East* (London, Richardson & Co, 1864)

Turnbull, C. M., *The Straits Settlements 1826–67: Indian Presidency to Crown Colony* (London, The Athlone Press, 1972)

Wurtzburg, Charles Edward, *Raffles of the Eastern Isles* (London, Hodder & Stoughton, 1954)

Articles

Clements, Sqn Ldr J., 'Isle of Peace, Blakang Mati – Island Fortress of Singapore' *Journal of the Royal Artillery,* Volume CVIII, No 2, September 1981

Firbank, Colonel L. T., 'A History of Fort Canning' (1950s, unpublished manuscript)

Harfield, Alan, 'Singapore Military Defences in the 19th Century', *Journal of the Society for Army Historical Research,* Volume 54, No 218, 1976

JMBRAS Volume XLII, Part 1, 'Singapore 150 Years', 1969

Kinross, John, 'The Fall of Singapore', *Fort* (Journal of the Fortress Study Group), No 37, 2009

Schmidtke, Dag, 'The British 9.2in BL Coast Defence Gun', *Casemate* (Journal of the Fortress Study Group), No 99, January 2014

Thomas, Gabriel, 'Fortress: A Military History of Blakang Mati Island' (National University of Singapore, unpublished thesis, 1996/7)

Yeoh, P. K., 'Fortress Singapore', *Fort* (Journal of the Fortress Study Group), No 7, 1979

Websites

C.C.M.Macleod-Carey
www.worldhistory.biz/world-warii/9324-c-c-m-macleod-carey.html

Report on Installations and Captured Weapons, Java and Singapore 1942 www.cgsc.contdtm.oclc.org

Singapore Coastal Defences
www.francefightson.yuku.com/topic/1412/SINGAPORE-COASTAL-DEFENCES

Peter Stubbs, Fort Siloso
www.fortsiloso.com

Raz Talkar, The Pengerang Battery
www.razcollection.com

Index

Page numbers in bold font denote an illustration or map within the text